ADHD
NOT JUST NAUGHTY

ABOUT THE AUTHOR

Elsie Bourke is a mother of three. Her eldest son CJ was diagnosed with ADHD at age seven after many problematic years. After that diagnosis, she made it her mission to learn all she could about ADHD in order to help her son.

She joined, then co-ran, a support group for parents of ADHD children, and was on call for those in need of support and a friendly ear.

Always having had a love of writing, she kept helpful reminder notes during this time, and these became the basis for this book – now written to help others on their own ADHD parenting journey.

Now also a proud nanna, Elsie lives on the Mornington Peninsula with her family.

"The diagnosis of ADHD can be seen as a blessing or a curse. The choice is yours."

ADHD *Not Just Naughty* is an uplifting guide for parents and caregivers of children diagnosed with Attention Deficit Hyperactivity Disorder (ADHD) as they navigate the rocky road of challenging behaviours. These include hyperactivity, impulsivity, inattention and often defiance.

This book recounts one mother's experiences, errors and successes in raising a son diagnosed with ADHD. If you find yourself often running on empty, unsure at times of which way to turn, and looking to restore your confidence, then this book is for you.

Practical parenting strategies are intertwined with real-life situations—the good, the bad and the ugly, with a dash of humour thrown in! Issues such as self-esteem, social skills, self-awareness, discipline and controlling anger are explored with a strong focus on the emotional well-being of both you and your child.

This book comes with a heartfelt message of hope, and that ADHD children are not *just naughty*. They are loving, intelligent, creative and unique little people with more potential than we realise. A diagnosis of ADHD can be a new beginning to a better relationship.

Dedication

To my dear son CJ, without whom this book would not have been written, proving a silver lining to whatever clouds may pass over us. To all of my family, much appreciation for putting up with my endless hours spent at the keyboard over the years. I am happy to say, there is finally a book!

******

Acknowledgement

A special thank you to Dr David Bannister, the caring paediatrician who diagnosed CJ's ADHD many years ago, and shone a hopeful light on the road ahead for which I am forever grateful.

ADHD
NOT JUST NAUGHTY

~

*One Mum's roadmap through the
early challenges of Attention Deficit
Hyperactivity Disorder*

E. H. BOURKE

plunge
PUBLISHING

ADVISORY NOTE:
We advise that the information contained in this book does not negate personal responsibility on the part of the reader for their own health and safety. It is recommended that individually tailored advice is sought from your healthcare or medical professional. The publisher and author are not liable for injuries or damage occasioned to any person as a result of reading or following the information contained in this book.

Some names in this book have been changed to protect the privacy of individuals.

First published 2018 by Plunge Publishing.
ISBN: 978-0-9954068-2-7 (paperback)
ISBN: 978-0-9954068-3-4 (ebook)
Plunge Publishing
PO Box 82,
Ringwood East,
VICTORIA,
Australia.
plungepublishing.com

A C.I.P. record for this book is available from the National Library of Australia.

CONTENTS

INTRODUCTION

Your fears have been confirmed! You've been given the diagnosis. Your child has Attention Deficit Hyperactivity Disorder (ADHD). For many parents, this is an unwelcome outcome, but it can also be seen as good news. You are not a bad parent, and your child isn't just 'a naughty child'. A diagnosis of ADHD isn't a life sentence but a new beginning. It's a starting point for a new phase in your life in which you learn to understand your child's challenging, and often frustrating, personality traits, and to revise your own parenting style to suit.

Of course, no parent wants their child labelled as different or having a 'disorder', but it doesn't have to be viewed that way. What you now have is the opportunity to gain knowledge; a key to understanding and a new beginning to a better relationship. You *can* make your home life easier, not by fighting against ADHD but by working with it. It's well within your power to take control and to make your family life calmer, happier and less exhausting.

Some parents may have a good handle on things and already cope well. But if you feel like you're often running on empty, unsure if you're heading in the right direction and looking for another perspective, then please read on. Within these pages, I hope to share with you many things I wish I'd known when I was a frazzled, first-time mother of a child with ADHD.

Initially, I had no understanding of why my son was so different from his more quiet and controlled playmates. My hope for him was to get through the day without creating at least some form of havoc, and to just see a smile on his little face. My aim was to get through the day with a smile on my own.

Fortunately, the diagnosis gave me some much-needed answers. It was time to stop comparing my son, CJ, to other children and to accept and appreciate his unique character traits. It was time to worry less about the opinions of others and to trust my own instincts. There was no doubt that dealing with ADHD would bring challenges, but it would be much less of a challenge with my son and I both working together. Through much trial and error, I did find my way.

My aim now is to help you find inner strength, inner peace, and different strategies to help you along your own path as you embark on your ADHD parenting journey. My hope is for you to better appreciate and enjoy your child, despite the challenges that ADHD brings. You should be prepared to stop for roadwork, to reassess and re-adjust, and to look for alternate routes. With time and patience, you will come to find a smoother road ahead. In relaying my stories and insights, errors and successes, I hope to help you envision a more positive future. There may not be instant results. Like a diet, one salad won't take off a kilo, but consistent commitment will bring a positive outcome.

Take heart. ADHD can also be an asset to our children with their many unique traits. They are spontaneous, imaginative, creative, energetic, resourceful and determined. Though often seemingly fearless and outspoken, this too can be an asset. I discovered this much later with CJ's persistence, confidence and boldness in the workforce as an adult, prepared to take calculated risks to reach his goals. Those with ADHD can utilise their unique character traits, to make exceptional leaders and ambitious employees, unafraid to stand up for what believe in. With a set goal in mind, they often forge right ahead when others would see only obstacles.

Right now, you may only see obstacles. You may feel as if you're fighting a losing battle, but you can change that with a resolve to let go of bad feelings from past experiences, to start fresh each day and to never give up. It's through the ability to 'never give up' that we achieve our success.

ADHD OVERVIEW

Attention Deficit Hyperactivity Disorder (ADHD) is a neurodevelopmental disorder that is said to affect approximately 7% of children. The average age of diagnosis is seven years old, and it is more commonly identified in boys than girls. Many adults are also now being diagnosed due to greater recognition of the disorder. The main characteristics are:

IMPULSIVITY

ADHD children act before they consider consequences, leading to reckless behaviour. They can't help touching, grabbing and blurting things out. They often appear rude by interrupting others and may speak inappropriately without regard to the effect their words have on others.

HYPERACTIVITY

They're always on the go and find it hard to settle down for quiet activities. They can't sit still for long or stand in line without fidgeting or moving. They may climb when unsafe to do so and run off without warning. They are often branded as the class clown or the 'naughty kid' for behaviours they find hard to control.

Inattention

They have a short attention span and struggle to hold concentration or tune out distractions.

Careless mistakes are made when they don't listen properly to instructions. They have difficulty staying on task, often moving to a new activity without finishing the first. They struggle with organisation and often misplace their belongings.

Inflexibility

They don't cope well with changes in their routine. They over-react to minor issues, which in turn, creates more significant problems. They may become easily frustrated and aggressive when things don't go their way. They often appear to be quite selfish but fail to see this in themselves.

Inconsistency

They often show considerable variation in the quality, speed and accuracy with which they perform tasks. A child may complete school work well one day but won't complete a similar project on a different day. This is often seen as laziness rather than as a trait of ADHD.

Immature Social Skills

ADHD children often have a younger emotional age than their peers, making it difficult for them to make and keep friends. Their frequently silly or aggressive behaviour is not well tolerated by more socially mature children. They will often play with children younger than themselves.

Poor Coordination

Poorly developed motor skills have a substantial effect on coordination and cause difficulty in doing simple tasks such as tying laces, riding a bike, or catching a ball. They may have difficulty with everyday skills that come readily to other children such as handwriting and organisational skills. The assistance of occupational therapy can be of benefit in developing their coordination.

Low Self-Esteem

ADHD children can be very sensitive, taking any negative comment to heart. They can feel anxious and discouraged and believe their efforts are never good enough. This can lead to other issues such as under-performing or becoming withdrawn and depressed.

POOR SHORT-TERM MEMORY

They often forget things that they recently learned or were shown and may require repeated instructions until they can finally store it in their long-term memory. They need constant reminders and reinforcement of correct behaviours.

LEARNING DIFFICULTIES

Most ADHD children have some type of learning difficulty. It could be a delay in reading, writing, spelling, maths or language. Parents may need to put in extra time at home to help their child cope. Those with a more severe learning disability may require the help of a teaching aide through their school's integration program.

SITUATIONAL VARIATION

Different situations can present a different child, with problems less noticeable during one-to-one activities compared to group situations. They can be better behaved when alone with one parent rather than with a family group. They will do better when activities are of greater interest to them, which is the reason that they can concentrate for an hour on a video game but not for five minutes to get dressed for school.

HOW IS ADHD DIAGNOSED?

ADHD children usually demonstrate problems at a young age. A diagnosis is generally made by studying a detailed history of the child's behaviours provided by parents, teachers and caregivers; and by utilising reliable checklists. This all helps to establish the persistence of the common traits and to what extent they are detrimentally affecting function in school, at home and socially. A comprehensive medical, behavioural and educational evaluation should be done, and a psychological assessment may also be necessary.

WHAT CAUSES ADHD?

The exact cause is unknown, but ADHD appears to have a firm biological basis and is seen to be hereditary in most cases. Many aspects remain a mystery, but research suggests a deficiency in specific neurotransmitters in the brain, adversely affecting function in the areas that control behaviour and concentration. ADHD is not caused by diet, but in some cases, dietary control including the avoidance of sugars, preservatives, food additives and colourings can be of benefit.

HOW CAN MEDICATION HELP?

Stimulant medications such as Ritalin and Adderall are not a cure for ADHD but have been found to substantially improve concentration and attention span and reduce impulsiveness in children that fulfil the ADHD criteria. While not a magic potion, medication enables a child to respond in a more 'normal manner' bringing benefits both academically and socially. There can be side effects including insomnia, loss of appetite, nausea and irritability. If side effects become a problem, a change of dosage or medication can be trialled, or medication may be ceased, as it is only a part of the management of ADHD.

WILL MY CHILD GROW OUT OF ADHD?

Many children will display their ADHD characteristics into adulthood but it is possible for them to 'outgrow' many of their negative traits. This comes through maturity, and by utilising effective management and organisational methods. Many traits can also be used to their advantage, such as creativity, persistence and a high energy level. However, some ADHD adolescents and adults will have problems with aggression, self-esteem, personal relationships and employment.

No one can predict a future, but early intervention

will ensure a head start by helping children to understand and manage their own behaviours as they grow into adulthood.

WHAT CAN PARENTS DO TO HELP?

Other strategies should always be used in conjunction with medication. Parents should be aware of their child's strengths and weaknesses and be prepared to assist where needed. ADHD children will make mistakes and have many obstacles to overcome. How they deal with situations relies heavily on the guidance, and the example set by parents and caregivers. ADHD children will need much understanding, praise, and encouragement in their home and school lives.

WHAT IS OPPOSITIONAL DEFIANCE DISORDER? (ODD)

Oppositional Defiance Disorder is a disorder that often presents in ADHD children. Symptoms include frequent arguing with adults, deliberately annoying others, refusing to comply with basic requests, rebelliousness, excessive anger, and blaming others for their misbehaviour. It can be present from an early age or develop over time, especially toward adolescence. ODD is far more than the expected normal range of these behaviours, and across multiple situations, such as at home, in school and social situations.

ADHD is now classified into three sub-types: predominately inattentive, predominately hyperactive-impulsive, and combined. Children with combined ADHD significantly demonstrate all three of these symptoms. This book is based around the combined sub-type of ADHD that affected my own son, and is most common.

1. MYSELF AND MY SON

I often wonder what I did to deserve such an irritable, disruptive, perplexing child. Most days are a battle from the moment he wakes up, with that almost permanent scowl on his little face, until he's finally back to sleep around 11 pm at night. He doesn't seem to care about anyone but himself and he's always angry about something. Each day when I pick him up from school, I have to mentally prepare myself for news of the silly, naughty things he's done that day. When he sees me, he's wearing that same scowl and, as always, something 'bad' has happened. By the time we get home, we end up in yet another pointless argument, sometimes both in tears. He yells that he hates me, and I could almost yell back the same. But I stop short of that because I do love him— more than he could ever imagine. I often ask myself, "Is this child really mine?"

I can honestly say that having a child with ADHD has made me a better person. I appreciate the small victories and joys—like just seeing a genuine smile on my son's face

1

or watching him playing happily with his younger brother and sister. With the diagnosis of ADHD, I had to rethink my priorities, learn to better control my emotions and my temper, and find new ways to deal with problem situations. I now understand why he behaves the way he does, even if I don't agree with it and have gained a new respect for his attempts to accomplish tasks which come more readily to most other children. In doing this, my son has, very slowly, followed this lead. Asked how his day was, the answer is usually 'good'. He still has his moments, and I have mine. There are still many problems to be faced, but they will be easier to overcome with us both on the same side.

So different are these two accounts, yet they were written by myself about the same child—my child! There was no miraculous overnight transformation but a gradual change. This change began with my own behaviour and reactions, which in turn, encouraged similar change in my son. The first account describes where many parents are today. The second describes where they can be, in the not so distant future.

Before my son CJ was diagnosed with ADHD, I had become withdrawn and embarrassed by his seemingly naughty and defiant behaviour. I was at a loss as to how to handle him or what to do to change his behaviour. It was like trying to drive through a strange city without a roadmap; constantly going around in circles, never knowing which way to turn and never quite reaching my destination. As a mother, I felt like a failure.

1987

Hip-hip-hooray! A beautiful son. Our first child, CJ, arrives. I started out with high expectations. He would be intelligent, polite and well-behaved just as I had been. We would be extremely close and have a special bond. He would be my greatest accomplishment. Or so I thought. I was totally unprepared for my actual reality. As an infant, he rarely slept more than two hours at a time, even after the first few months. His daytime sleeps wore off fast, and it was difficult to get anything done at home. Still, I loved my little bundle of joy to bits, tired as I always was, and I assumed that all babies were like this.

Determined to do everything right, I took my new-mummy role seriously. I read the popular parenting books, joined a playgroup, read CJ bedtime stories, sang to him, and took him for walks in his pram, but nothing was quite as I had expected. As a toddler, he'd refuse to hold my hand, and at the first opportunity, he would make his escape. He would run off, glancing back at me with a cheeky grin, like a puppy with a prized stolen sock, ready for the chase.

In the playground, he would push other children if they annoyed him, and getting him to share seemed as appealing to him as asking him to pull his own hair out by the roots. As he grew, he became loud and boisterous, often at the worst possible times. He was the absolute opposite of my quiet, introverted self.

I would reason with him, explain things in detail, and when necessary, use timeout for punishments (as suggested in those days), but this so-called 'normal parenting' just didn't seem to work. He would shout at the top of his lungs if sent to his room as a punishment, and 'no' soon became his favourite word.

CJ's first trouble with authority (aside from mine!) was at the age of two and a half when he was suspended from our local playgroup for his lone instigation of what I dubbed 'The Great Table-Tipping Incident of 1989'. Happy-faced children sat quietly on small plastic chairs, at a small plastic table, drawing colourful pictures. CJ wandered over, quietly watching them.

All seemed calm when, without warning, CJ suddenly tipped the table over with a loud thud! A rainbow of pencils, crayons and cheerful stick-figure drawings flew onto the floor. Children screamed and mothers wearing disapproving looks ran over to comfort them. CJ smiled cheekily, seemingly pleased with his handiwork. Horrified and embarrassed, I hurriedly cleaned up, attempting to apologise through a thick veil of parental shame. I then took my 'little terror' home and did the only thing there was to do. I cried.

CJ didn't seem too fussed about the whole episode, but from that time on, I knew I'd have to grow eyes in the back of my head and maybe on each side as well. Had he not been my first child, I may have felt differently with a 'regular one' under my belt, but as a first-time mum and knowing no different, I blamed myself. I wondered what I was doing wrong.

Not long after, I took CJ to the local health nurse to discuss my concerns. She told me to leave him playing in the toy/waiting room while we talked. Though this lack of supervision made me uneasy, she assured me it was quite child-proof, and he couldn't get into any trouble there.

The health nurse listened intently as I related incidents that, to me seemed out of the ordinary for a child of CJ's age. At the conclusion of my well-rehearsed speech, she told me to relax, that this was perfectly normal for boys. She had a son, and he was exactly the same.

Of course! All my friends had daughters. Most of his cousins were also girls. Nice, quiet girls. At that moment, it sounded like a reasonable explanation—
he was just a boy!

Feeling pleased and somewhat relieved, I went back to the toy room to collect CJ, but was confronted by a mass of coloured paper covering the floor. It took me a few moments to realise that CJ had taken all of the pamphlets from the information stand and strewn them around the room (quite happily too—by the look on his satisfied little face).

I spent the next half hour sorting out leaflets covering subjects from breast examination to depression. I thought that the pamphlet on depression might come in handy, and I wondered if I had seen the real health nurse or whether she was just a figment of my imagination to temporarily allay my fears! (I later learnt that, unbeknown to her at that time, her own son had ADHD, so she had considered my concerns and CJ's behaviours as 'normal')

The kindergarten year seemed to go well with CJ fitting in as well as any four-year-old. He was quite the happy-chappy, still a live-wire but much the same as many of the other boys. I felt quietly confident and looked forward to when he would begin school, certain that it would stimulate him and settle him down. He would have a caring teacher who would take him under her wing and see the sweet, intelligent boy behind the silly behaviour ... but alas I was wrong.

The first two years of school were what could only be called 'nightmare years'. His first teacher was very strict, with no time for silliness. CJ would protest most mornings when we arrived at the school gate, begging me not to send him in. I would wait until after the bell when he was safely in the classroom; then I would leave despondently, worrying about him for the rest of the school day. In the next two years, he became noisy and disruptive, constantly in trouble and not learning much at all. Unsuspectingly, this was his way of saying 'I need help'. No-one could hear his cry, not even me.

He was soon branded 'one of the naughty kids', and in those first school years, he lost his self-esteem and his innocence. He became moody and sullen. I took him to different doctors for advice. "Oh, he'll grow out of it," or "he's a typical boy," they'd say. As he grew older and no better behaved, I'd be asked carefully: "What's your home situation like? Maybe you're too tense. Do you spank him?"… All my fault, they seemed to be suggesting. By this time, my own self-esteem had plummeted. I felt silently criticised, often getting haughty looks from other parents at school pick-up. I soon became reluctant to be around other mums with their well-behaved children. I felt alone, even with friends around me. By then CJ's dad, Bob, was also struggling to deal with him, and with Bob working long hours, the parenting and 'problem solving' were generally left to me.

Sometimes at night, in the darkness of his room after a bedtime story, I would catch a glimpse of the sweet little boy inside the defiant exterior. CJ would say something 'normal' and loving, as if he was trying to 'break through', but in a flash, it would be gone, and the silliness would return. I would leave his room with an overwhelming sadness for what my son and we—his family—were missing out on.

By the age of seven, CJ was a big brother to sister Shari, then five, and a new baby brother Harry. CJ was a very loving brother, but not a lot had changed with his general attitude. He still mostly disliked school, but outwardly seemed to be getting by. However, after one particularly bad day at school, with CJ finding himself in trouble yet again, a distressing incident occurred, one that came to be our most defining moment.

We were in the kitchen getting after-school snacks and talking about the goings-on of the day when CJ grabbed a large kitchen knife. He turned it toward himself and yelled that he might as well not be here because everybody hates him and everything he does is wrong.

Horrified I took the knife from him, hugged him and told him everything would be okay, but having no idea if it would be or not. It took me until that point to admit to myself that there was something seriously wrong and that CJ needed more help than I knew how to give.

Devastated that our son was in such torment, I did the only thing I could think of—I went to the library (there was no Google back then!). That day, after much searching, I found a lifeline—a book about hyperactive children, and there was CJ, described to a tee: impulsive, overactive and inattentive. The list went on.

That day I found the name of a recognised disorder: Attention Deficit Hyperactivity Disorder. The jigsaw puzzle of seemingly random and unrelated traits had come together enabling me to see the bigger picture. At last, I had found a turning point and somewhere to begin. I thanked the heavens.

I consulted a paediatrician, Dr Bannister. (I'd seen a flyer with his name on it in the doctor's office once.) At that time, he worked with many ADHD children and their families. He confirmed my suspicions and gave me hope—hope, finally, for a better future. I soon realised that things were never going to be as I had expected, so it was time to readjust and make a fresh start. It was to be our new beginning. I knew I had to learn all that I could about this 'ADHD' if I were to help my son.

I began to change tactics and gradually work on my own parenting style. It was time to trust myself to find new strategies that would work with my very hyperactive but very much-loved son. Tentatively, I joined a support group and met some wonderful parents, many with far worse issues than ours. Just being able to talk, laugh and sometimes cry with other parents that had similar issues was a great support. I eventually came to co-run the support group and became more confident in my own abilities. This was a great benefit to CJ and our family as a whole.

Even though things became a little easier, I would still have bad days with CJ, and I'd ask myself, "How can I possibly give advice when look at me today? I'm a sooky mess!" But, I'd remind myself that I could learn from these 'bad' days, work out what I could have done differently and choose to try new tactics in the future.

I began to keep a notebook for myself of what worked and what didn't, finding solutions through much trial and error. These notes became my ADHD roadmap—my own personal reminders to keep me positive, to remind me to take my own advice when I was feeling down, and to remind me that I was indeed a good mother. When I felt lost, I'd pick up my notes, redirect myself and soon be back on my way. I realised that I could decide how I wanted our lives to be and aim for that life.

TRAVEL TIPS:

- Believe in yourself—believe in your child.
- Trust your instincts—they're usually right.
- You have the power to change your life.

2. ACCEPTANCE

"It's only when we refuse to bend, that we break."

A diagnosis of ADHD comes with many conflicting emotions. Some embrace the diagnosis, grateful for some type of answer. Others are disappointed, downhearted or resentful. It's easy to get depressed and angry at the world. It's easy to lay blame on others.

"The doctors should have diagnosed earlier, teachers should have picked up on it, my partner is exactly the same, so it must be his fault!' or 'my in-laws just don't understand and are too hard on him."

These are just some of the ways we can lay blame. Ultimately, this attitude is pointless and will work against us. While we may be justified in passing off some this blame, it only colours our thoughts in a negative way.

For me, the discovery that CJ had ADHD brought out mixed emotions. I was grateful for this new starting point, yet apprehensive for what lay ahead. I found the most effective way to deal with these conflicting emotions, was to get myself into the right mind frame. I had to make a conscious effort to accept that CJ had a recognised medical issue and to treat it as such.

It can be very daunting at first, when we're more

prone to working against the traits and behaviours that come with ADHD, than working with them. That said, there's not one thing we can do to change the fact that our child has ADHD. We can lament the unfairness of it, wish it wasn't so, or forever ask, "Why me?" but it won't make one bit of difference.

On difficult days, I would often ask myself, "Why me?" But I came to realise that the answer was there all the time, and that answer was — 'because you are the best person to raise this child'. I had to believe in that. There was no other choice. Ask yourself that same question and give yourself that same answer. We can't change the hand we've been given, but we can work to improve our situation with the knowledge we now have.

KEEP A 'SPECIAL NEEDS' PERSPECTIVE

Even though it can't be visibly seen, ADHD is still very real, and children's difficulties need to be accepted and accommodated. We wouldn't tell a sight-impaired child to look harder, and we wouldn't tell a hearing-impaired child to listen better. We would assist them with various 'tools', such as a hearing aid, sign language, glasses or a guide dog. As ADHD manifests mainly as a behavioural problem, we can't just say, "Be good". What we can do is to provide our children with the tools they need to succeed. We already have in our possession one of the best tools we can give them, and that is setting a good example for them to follow, with our actions, our attitude, and our acceptance of this new road to be travelled.

When we accept that a child's apparently naughty behaviour is mainly due to their ADHD (I say 'mainly' because they don't get off the hook quite that easily!), we become calmer, more focused and ready for whatever lies ahead. It becomes easier to offer positive and effective correction instead of just seeing a badly-behaved child that needs to be pulled into line. More than anything our ADHD kids need help, encouragement and reassurance, not criticism and condemnation. Without doubt, they will face enough of that elsewhere.

We don't have to take every challenging behaviour personally, but that's exactly what I did for a long time. I often felt as if CJ was trying to sabotage my parenting, and that misguided mindset was the reason life became so stressful. I was letting emotions get in the way of rational thinking. I adored CJ. He was clever, funny and loving though he frustrated me no end at times, and I came to realise that the things that most annoyed or upset me were just behaviours. Behaviours can be changed, and that change began with me. By accepting the way things were, then changing my own thoughts, actions and reactions I could begin to change CJ's negative attitude, actions and reactions that had become everyday occurrences.

APPLES AND ORANGES

Even at age seven CJ would rarely dress himself or get ready for school without an exhausting performance of complaint about how it was so unfair, how it was too early to get dressed. He would ask, "What's wrong with staying in pyjamas?" or simply say, "Leave me alone." I would start off being patient, but then I would think about our next-door neighbour's child of the same age who dressed herself every morning, was sensible, caring and seemed like the perfect child. I would start comparing and suddenly become angry. It just wasn't fair! But it was my own thoughts comparing the two that was making me angry, not so much the actual situation. I was comparing two totally different children, like apples and oranges. When I accepted that CJ's behaviour was perfectly normal for a child with ADHD, and not a conscious attempt to get on my nerves, it was much easier to stay calm and in control. I knew that soon he wouldn't want me to dress him. It wasn't going to be a long-term issue, and if I helped him for few minutes, it would save time for all of us. I was making a big deal about a small aggravation when there would be many more important issues to overcome. Though one day I did start to drive him to school in his pyjamas and he quick-smart changed his tune - and the pyjamas!

The dreaded M word

One of the things I found most difficult to accept was the realisation that I was going to be placing my son on medication. When CJ was five, I saw a news item which featured hyperactive children that had been put on a drug, Ritalin. I remember looking at CJ who was plainly boisterous and challenging, not knowing that he too would have this diagnosis. I wondered how a parent could ever do that. I couldn't imagine giving a child a drug to calm him down. It was only when CJ became more troubled and withdrawn, rather than just hyperactive, and was having much difficulty in school, that I came to do the same. It was not to make my life easier, but to improve his life — personally, academically and socially.

After the initial visits and testing, our paediatrician, Dr Bannister, suggested a trial of medication. To say I was extremely hesitant is a huge understatement, yet there I was, getting a prescription filled for Ritalin. At that point, I was ready to try almost anything. I still remember the moment I first gave it to him. I felt so guilty and worried that it would make him sick, or turn him into a zombie, but my fears were unfounded. It worked well. CJ had a renewed spark in him. Finally, the glimpses of normality became regular occurrences. He became easier to talk to and actually paid attention. And he was happier. And he was calmer.

It was as if he'd had an inner accelerator pedal that had been stuck on full speed ahead and Ritalin gave him his brakes, even if only temporarily.

One of the most profound differences his medication made was in his handwriting. It went from almost illegible to totally acceptable for his year level. It was as if his hands had been untied. But best of all he began to smile more, and that in itself, deserved a trumpet and fanfare. Medication alone would not be the answer, but we had accepted that it could be a part of the solution.

EMBRACE THE DIFFERENT

'Different' isn't bad. It just might mean we have to work harder for an improved result and change some of our well-worn parenting beliefs to accommodate the uniqueness of our families. Some may say, "Why should I? Children are expected to behave," but it's helpful to remember that our ADHD children are often as frustrated as we are when things don't turn out the way they expected. They usually think they're behaving just fine and have no idea that their behaviour isn't acceptable to the rest of the world until they find themselves 'in trouble'. They're usually more immature and less self-aware than their peers, so they need much love and understanding as they usually don't love or understand themselves.

Some may say, "We do more than enough already! We're pushed to the limit. We've tried everything!" and it may be true to a point, but we have never done absolutely everything. When we accept this, we can get on with the job. Far worse things can happen to us in this life than to have a child with ADHD. Ask any parent who has had to bear the heartbreaking loss of a child. They would have them back in a millisecond, whatever way they came. We're lucky. We have our kids here safe with us, and we have a lot to work with.

Various forms of ADHD manifest differently in our children. Some may be more talkative, some more withdrawn, some more hyperactive. They can seem very different from each other just like any other children, but there's always that common thread running through them, that sense of 'you never quite know what will happen next'…

One afternoon I took seven-year-old CJ and his younger sister, Shari, to do the grocery shopping. As he'd behaved so well that morning, I didn't give CJ any medication, forgetting his questionable shopping excursion behaviours of the past. While I waited at the checkout, CJ began to race up and down an aisle at high speed with his little sister laughing as she clung to the side of a trolley, but at the same time, clearly in fear for her life! Disapproving customers looked sternly at my son as if he were the devil possessed. Normally, my first impulse would have been to panic and yell at him, but it occurred to me that this was typical CJ behaviour (though silly and dangerous!) due to his typical ADHD traits. He thought this was quite a fine thing to do. 'Old me' would have been angry and embarrassed, but 'new me' had a good understanding of his thought process and actions. In his eyes, it was a just bit of fun, some sibling bonding, and he was doing this right in front of me, so he obviously didn't think I'd be angry with him. An outburst by me would have just caused a scene, added more stress and done no good at all. Instead, I hurried over, taking control of the trolley-turned-race car and told CJ that I needed his help to take out our bags. Safely in the car, I then explained the danger in his actions. Because there was no conflict situation, he actually took notice of what I said. Fortunately, there was no repeat performance, and on the next shopping trip, I made sure to give him his medication. There soon came a time though, when I could send him into a supermarket on his own with a list of items, knowing I could trust him and that he would be fine.

ADVANTAGE ADHD

It may not seem obvious right now, but ADHD children have definite advantages. They have boundless energy that can be directed into worthwhile pursuits (not just having their parents chase after them!). They can have incredible concentration on an activity that interests them (room cleaning, teeth cleaning and getting dressed do not interest them!). They're open to being creative and spontaneous when the opportunity arises (and also when it doesn't!) They are unique individuals that come up with new ideas and think outside the box—when they're not climbing on top of it! That said, they are also like any other child: loving, intelligent, caring, fun-loving and able to fill our lives with love and joy.

When a child is created nature/genetics make certain decisions over which we have no control, like sex, eye colour, hair colour or height. Brains can be wired differently too. Who is to say what's normal? I often think that back in cave-man days, CJ would have been a brave leader, taking the initiative, fearlessly hunting ferocious prey for the tribal meal. He'd fight off enemies without considering his own safety (or that of others!). He'd lead a scouting party through rugged terrain and go where 'no man had gone before' (especially, if his mother told him not to!).

Understandably the orderly routine of school or any quiet, structured activity is not always the place for this boldness and abundance of energy, and that's where things start to go awry and they find themselves 'in trouble'. But given a chance, ADHD children are intelligent, creative, unique individuals with imaginative minds and a huge capacity to make their mark on the world.

Even though ADHD is termed a disorder, it's one that can be worked with. Through time, patience and loving guidance, it can often be turned into an asset. Take, for example, business magnate and Virgin Founder Sir Richard Branson, actor/producer Jim Carey, singer/actor Justin Timberlake, multi-medal winning Olympian swimmer Michael Phelps, celebrity chef Jamie Oliver, author and Pulitzer Prize winner Katherine Ellison, actor Michelle Rodriguez and comedian/actor/writer/producer, the late Joan Rivers, just to name a few. These people are all celebrated in their fields, with their ADHD not a hindrance to their success, but very often an advantage to it. Whether our children become famous or not, it's encouraging to know that ADHD doesn't have to be a deterrent to their happiness or to their potential.

Ultimately a child's ADHD will be their own responsibility. Eventually, we can' 'walk away' and leave them to live their own life, so it's vital we give them the best start and the skills to enable them to lead a happy and successful adulthood. Working in harmony with your child's personality, accepting both their shortcomings and their gifts, will guide you on your way.

Accept that you will have to take a slightly different road on the journey of parenthood. There will be times we reach a dead end, times we need to make an unexpected U-turn or times we just have to stop, turn our motors off and recharge our batteries.

Each night as I close my eyes I say the Serenity Prayer to myself. To me, this is the epitome of acceptance. (Initially, I had no idea it was the AA motto, but that may have come in handy!)

> *God grant me the serenity*
> *to accept the things I cannot change,*
> *the courage to change the things I can,*
> *and the wisdom to know the difference.*
>
> *Reinhold Niebuhr*

In these few lines, it's as if I've put a lid on any troubles of today and prepared my mind, fresh for tomorrow. I can fall asleep with a hopeful expectancy of good things to come. We all want to have peace of mind and to be able to give that to ourselves is one the greatest gifts.

TRAVEL TIPS:

- Accept and embrace your child's unique personality.
- Accept and embrace unexpected detours to find your way.
- Accept and embrace that you are the best person to raise this child.

3. UNDERSTANDING

"ADHD—When arguing means negotiating. When climbing is an effective mode of transport. When grabbing impatiently is just testing things out first. When being silly is selflessly entertaining others. When making friends equals 'What's wrong with me?' When trying your best never seems good enough. ADHD—When understanding means a world of difference."

Imagine you're in a strange country. You don't know the customs or understand the culture. You might have a reasonable idea, but some things you just don't 'get' yet. It might be using chopsticks instead of a fork, or you might have trouble remembering that arriving on time is considered rude in your host country. You might inadvertently offend by giving a 'thumbs up' in a country where it's considered rude. You may need to be shown or reminded over and over again of the correct etiquette, and still make mistakes, even with your best intentions. You might never adapt enough to pass as a local, but you would hope that people would accept your best efforts to fit in.

Our ADHD kiddies can feel alienated from other children who aren't as impulsive or as boisterous as themselves and feel as if they don't fit in. This doesn't mean that they never will, it just means they will need extra help along the way. Alternatively, they may see no difference and wonder why they are often left out or avoided. They may either be oblivious to their differences or acutely aware of them. Either situation presents its own challenges.

FULL SPEED AHEAD

Imagine that we have gears which we use to manoeuvre through our day. Slow, to medium, to fast, at ever-changing speeds depending on what we're doing. Slow for morning coffee, medium as we start our chores and faster as we rush off to work. Our ADHD kids predominately use just one gear, and that's full speed ahead! It would be like trying to manoeuvre a car around corners doing 100 kms an hour. Not an easy feat and they're bound to have some crashes along the way. So, think of yourself as parental roadside assistance, with a dash of love thrown in.

When we take the time to understand the traits of ADHD we realise that they have little control over many of their frustrating behaviours. When we try to 'step into their shoes' to understand how they feel, we will see that they can't change their 'make-up,' but that we can help them to be more aware of themselves, of their feelings and of their behaviours.

Imagine having to sit still and stay quiet for three hours. What a mammoth effort we'd have to make to achieve this, if we could at all! Eventually, we'd become fidgety and impatient. We would most likely give in and get out of our seat at the very least. That's how it can feel to a hyperactive child when they need to sit quietly for fifteen minutes, but the fidgeting and impatience will come almost immediately!

INADVERTENT INATTENTION

Most ADHD behaviours that we find annoying are done without conscious thought. To say stop fidgeting to our ADHD child is like telling ourselves to stop blinking. We could try for a moment, but couldn't possibly keep it up. It isn't a conscious decision to fidget; it just happens, like blinking. If there's no harm done, ignore it and let it pass. It can be hard to ignore behaviours when we feel our child isn't trying, is acting in a silly way or causing a scene; but they don't plan to be annoying or forgetful, or the class clown. These behaviours are often the only way a child can cope and are often their way of saying, "I just want to fit in".

Imagine trying to concentrate on something important like your tax return or studying for a test with the TV blaring loudly in the room, doors banging, and your phone ringing, all at the same time. It would be almost impossible! This is what it can feel like to our ADHD children when trying to work in the classroom. There may be a bird at the window, another child asking a question, another student going to the bathroom, but for our kiddies, everything is magnified, creating a loss of concentration and distraction, usually followed by being 'in trouble'.

Speaking of distractibility, as I was writing a sentence in this chapter I looked at my gloved hand and realised I'd come inside to get the shed key, but here I was in front of my laptop. I'd had a 'book-thought' to add in and I found myself sitting here typing. After a moment, I wondered, "What was I supposed to be doing?" Then I remembered, "Oh, yes—the shed key!" Writing down that must-have-been-so-important book-thought was on impulse, and before I knew it, I'd totally forgotten what I was actually doing (still not sure why I was wearing the glove!).

We all do it—we walk into a room and think, what are we doing here? It's not just our ADHD children that get side-tracked. Imagine if this was how it was for you all day long. You go to put away some clean washing then find yourself trying on a kaftan and some gold boots that you came across in your wardrobe … (oops, wasn't I meant to be doing laundry?) Luckily, no one is going to come in and tell us off. We're grown-ups right … but this is the same thing our little ADHD offspring are often 'in trouble' for.

Rather than reprimanding them, help them with a smile. "Hey, sweetheart. Aren't you supposed to be getting me your homework book?" as he looks up from his Big Book of Monster trucks. "Oh, yeah.

Thanks, Mum," and he's back on task. Using love, understanding and kindness rather than reprimands that make them feel inferior will give a better and calmer outcome.

We all have some ADHD traits at times. We too can be impulsive, stubborn or distractible but to a lesser extent, and with the difference being that we can learn by example and through reflection to control these traits. We can be objective about ourselves when we need to be, and in hindsight, we can see how we may have looked to others. Our children don't have this objectivity or hindsight and can be blind to how their behaviour and words affect others.

FILTER FAIL

We all have negative thoughts, but as adults, we're (usually) much better at filtering what we say. We may be thinking the same thing as someone with ADHD, but the difference is that we usually won't come out and say it because we know it isn't acceptable. One way to envisage this is how we feel and react to situations after two glasses of wine (or whatever your tipple!).

Our filters become less stable, and we get louder, less inhibited, and we begin to say more than we usually would. We're more likely to say or do things we wouldn't normally because our impulses aren't properly regulated. Imagine being this impulsive in everyday life and having to make a concentrated effort to contain your words and actions. Imagine that every thought you had sprung forth from your mouth before you had time to consider it. This is how it can be for our ADHD children. For us, in retrospect, we may feel a bit embarrassed and regretful; but our children don't have this reflection because it's how their impulses are all the time. There's no 'sobering up' effect—no afterward to think about what they said, with the possible exception of when they are on their medication. They rarely see anything wrong with their words or behavior.

"Hi Auntie Caroline. Your hair looks awful today, what did you do to it?" or *"Yuck, Grandma. Dinner is horrible".*

The thought is born and instantly emerges with no filtering process to stop it. Most of us have seen the movie 'Liar Liar' and thought it was hilarious when Jim Carrey's character could only speak the truth, but imagine if this was your real life. It's not so funny then and won't always have the happy ending.

Strangely enough, telling the truth (their truth) can be what teaches our children to lie, because they are so often in trouble for saying exactly what they think. They soon learn to make things up as a way of self-preservation to hopefully stay out of trouble. Then it becomes a habit, and we wonder why they lie.

The words disorder and disability are often used in regard to ADHD, but there are so many things in life that can be a 'disability,' such as being selfish, being dishonest, being too nice or even just being shy. All these things can impact our lives negatively, but can be changed with understanding and self-awareness, just like many of our children's problem traits.

When I was young, I was extremely shy. I found it very difficult to have any sort of a normal conversation. I couldn't speak up in class even when I had something valid to contribute. It was debilitating, and it did become in a way, a disability to me. My only asset was a reasonably good sense of humour. So, I would say something funny, rather than join in the conversation. The other students would laugh, and I was, in a small way, accepted.

How I would have loved to be able to interact as the other students did, but I didn't have the skills. I couldn't just decide not to be shy, just as our ADHD children can't say "Okay I won't be hyperactive or inattentive". These are, of course, entirely different issues but showcase similar ways of coping. ADHD children often just muddle through the best as they can, as I did. They are often the jokers or the pranksters, not because they want to be naughty, but because they want to be accepted and making others laugh can be their 'secret weapon' in their quest to fit in. The problem is that parents and teachers aren't laughing.

Think of a habit or characteristic of your own that you'd like to change. Even as adults we struggle to alter our own habits and character traits. We have first to be aware of them, and then make a conscious effort to change them, and it's not always easy. We might try to improve our diet or speak more clearly, chew more quietly or not butt into conversations (yes, admittedly these are all mine!). Unsurprisingly, even when we have this self-awareness and know what we need to do, it can still be difficult to alter our behaviours. Imagine how hard it is for a child who has little self-awareness or little concept as to how his behaviours affect others. To them, their behaviour is perfectly normal, and they're often confused as to why they should change, or how they end up in that frequently-visited place—that second-home called 'trouble'.

KNOWLEDGE IS KEY

We're fortunate in that we know our ADHD children lack in many basic skills. We can help them to learn more acceptable behaviours in many small ways by offering everyday examples and directly explaining the ways of the world with love and patience.

With the beginning of school life, CJ began to

lose his self-esteem and became moody and sullen. We began to see less of the sweet, trusting child that he should have been…that he used to be. Why did we rarely see this side of him? Because he didn't know how he was supposed to act. His brain told him one thing while the rest of the world, including me, told him something entirely different. He was constantly seen as 'the naughty kid' for just being himself. If it was a social disability like shyness, where you have a good awareness of the sort of person you want to be and what you need to try and change, it can be more easily addressed, but our ADHD children have little or no self-awareness, so they can't just help themselves.

They might have a tantrum before school and shout that they hate going to school! In frustration, we might reply something like, "Well, bad luck. You're going, and that's that!" Alternatively, we can take a few moments, show that we care and let them know that we're on their side. If we just ask a few questions, we can gain a better understanding and be able to reassure our child that things will be okay— that school will be okay. A few minutes of paying attention to their needs can save half an hour of sulking or arguing.

It's important to ask a child what's really going on. It may seem to go without saying, but often we have no idea. Ask specific questions and listen. "Why do you feel sad? What is making you feel angry?" Offer suggestions. "Are you worried about the cross country today? Did you have homework due? Is there a problem with another child in your class?" Ask what you can do to help. "Would you like to me come in and talk to the teacher with you?"

It could be something as simple as a sports day, and they think they'll be the slowest runner. We can point out that not everyone can be the fastest, and that we'll be proud of them just for doing their best. There's no better they can do. Just knowing they've been listened to and acknowledged will help them to feel validated and more open to listening to your point of view. Maybe you can't help, but you can just be there in the moment. Then there's always that good old fallback—the hug! A hug can be a mood lifter, a trust builder, a stress reliever, instant calm and the best natural medicine.

We often think strict is best, but it isn't always. Neither is too lax. So, find that middle ground. Self-regulation will come with maturity and with a loving learning atmosphere in which to grow. It may not be easy, but it can be done successfully if we take it one day at a time, one hour at a time, even one minute at a time if we must. The objective is to find a way to live in harmony with ADHD instead of in a battle against it. Otherwise, our children will just rebel or withdraw further into their tough little shells. We may never fully hold the reins with our ADHD children, but we can hold those reins with them: together as a team, through acceptance, understanding, positivity and love.

TRAVEL TIPS:

- Step into your child's shoes. Imagine how they feel.
- Remember: they don't want to be 'the naughty one'.
- Try the two glasses of wine comparison (and call it research!).

4. EXPECTATIONS

"Low expectations can be self-fulfilling prophecies, high expectations—pressure cookers. Flexible, realistic expectations—a middle ground, a place in which to thrive."

We all have hopes, dreams and expectations for our children. We hope that they will be happy and healthy; we dream that they will have success at school and in their adult lives; we expect that they will fit perfectly into our family unit and bring us much joy. But what happens is not always what we expect. There are no guarantees of perfection or any promises that parenting will be easy. My own expectations for CJ slowly diminished during his first seven years. While other parents may hope for their child to have great sporting abilities, be an excellent speller or a maths whiz, my wishes were much more modest. I hoped that one day CJ would wait patiently in a line, answer when I called him, and not fight with every child at a birthday party. My big hope was that he would just be happy.

FOR BETTER OR WORSE

Every child is unique. Some are going to be easier to raise—some more difficult, but all are precious.

None belong in the 'too hard basket'. Even more so than in a marriage, we care for our children 'for better, for worse, in sickness and in health', so it's important that we adjust ourselves and our expectations accordingly. Our ADHD children may need extra care and guidance, but they still bring, as expected, much joy, laughter and happy unpredictability into our lives.

Imagine you're getting a new pet. You've decided you might like a rabbit—soft and adorable. You'd feed him daily, clean out his cage weekly, play with him occasionally and that's about it—but what you come home with is a puppy, soft and adorable also, but that's where the similarity ends. He needs to be fed, bathed, walked and trained. He will chase your cat, rip the towels off the line and dig up your petunias. He will pee on your carpet, whine all night and want constant attention, but *you know* that all puppies behave this way. This is what to expect. You might get advice from the vet. You might take him to puppy school. You will do your best to mould him into the type of dog you want him to be, knowing that when he is grown, it will all have been worth it. You may not have your low-maintenance rabbit but caring for that puppy, while much more time consuming, will be greatly rewarding.

The same may be said of our ADHD children, and no I'm not really comparing a child to a pet as such, but you get the idea. It's to be expected that our ADHD children will have difficulties with simple everyday things that come easily to other children, and they may need more of our time. They will need to be constantly motivated to do the right thing and have their fragile self-esteem constantly boosted. It may sound difficult, but it becomes easier when we adjust our expectations according to our children's individual personalities and accept them, rather than trying to suppress them.

Most mornings at breakfast, CJ would rock up and down in his chair as if trying to manoeuvre it around like a primitive mode of transport. He would jiggle about, shake his head back and forth, and sing loud, nonsensical songs. It was as if he was trying his best to be deliberately annoying, to see how much he could push my buttons. In hindsight, it was just CJ being CJ, nothing personal. I was continually telling him to stop, and I was getting myself worked up about it. He'd stop for about three seconds, laugh and then start again. I would eventually lose my patience and yell at him. He would yell back that I hated him, storm off and do nothing after that without an argument. This made for a very stressful start to the day for both of us, so things had to change if we were to keep our relationship intact.

Do What Works for You

I knew that he couldn't control these impulses to a large extent. He was hyperactive after all. I knew that this was exactly the type of behaviour to expect from a child with ADHD. I could choose to work against his natural trait or to work with it. I chose the latter. Unsure of where exactly to start, I could at least try to handle the situation differently. If what I was doing wasn't working, then there was no harm in trying another approach.

At first, I decided to ignore him as best as I could. I told him that it was okay to sing as long as he didn't rock in the chair, adding that he might fall off. That worked for a while, but he was still loud, so I would leave briefly and do something else—make a bed or put on some washing. This temporary change of scenery would diffuse any looming confrontation. Also, CJ didn't seem to enjoy his shenanigans as much without an audience. Some days I would just pop in earplugs (he never knew this) and I stopped allowing myself to get worked up about the noise. After all, it was only for about twenty minutes each morning. He soon became a little quieter, and I came to see that much of his behaviour was exaggerated because I made such an issue of it. I had allowed a small annoyance to become much bigger than it needed to be.

CJ's behaviour was fairly normal for a child with ADHD, and the sooner I prepared myself for what to expect, the better a parent I could be to him. I could expect that:

- He would speak inappropriately, *but* I could give him alternatives.
- He would be overactive, *but* I could find

suitable activities for his energy.

- He would have learning difficulties, *but* I could give him help and support.
- He would make mistakes, *but* I could give him a second chance.
- He would have bad days, *but* I'd be there to listen and care.

KEEP A HEALTHY DETACHMENT

Our children will have bad days, but their problems don't have to become our problems. We can be there to listen, offer a hug or advice and sometimes just to let them be. After school, there was generally a big drama that CJ had to tell me about. I'd hear all the annoying, unfair things that happened to CJ during the day (both real and imagined) within the first three minutes of getting in the car. Just one day can't it be good news?

Immediately, I'd feel stressed. I'd sigh. I'd listen. I'd offer solutions. I'd criticise. I'd judge. I'd feel all the emotion of the situations he'd encountered as if I was there too. I'd become annoyed at CJ and also angry at the alleged perpetrators. I was then an active part of the perceived drama. But I didn't have to be a part of it. It didn't have to become my problem. Instead of taking it personally, I could keep a healthy detachment. I could listen to him with an open mind, acknowledge his feelings and let him know that I was there for him.

Often, as parents, we think that we need to be responsible for everything that happens to our children and fix it: that we must find all the answers. In a serious situation, yes, maybe; but an ADHD child's day can be full of imagined looks and wrongly perceived situations. There are dramas that will never unfold and problems so minor they don't need solving. We shouldn't take everything as gospel, or to heart.

Expect that your child will exaggerate or have a very different perception of events compared to what really happened. Let them have their say, get all their negative feelings out of their system. Listen and acknowledge these feelings, but don't become emotionally involved. Just be there, with an open ear, an open heart and an open mind and they will probably have forgotten any school day dramas by the time they get out of the car and go in the front door at home.

EXPECT THEIR BEST AS BEST AS YOU CAN

We can also expect too little, giving children self-limiting beliefs that hold them back. We might say in front of them, "Oh, Daniel can't sit still for that long," or "Sarah's writing is always terrible," or "it's probably Jack's fault, he's always in trouble". They come to believe this is their identity; that this is what people expect of them, and they behave accordingly.

We might think they never listen, but their little ears pick up on many things that we think they are oblivious to.

While recognising the negatives, we're also entitled to expect a child's best. There are many things that they *can* control, and ADHD isn't a 'get out of jail free' card.

We can expect that they will:
- help at home—try their best;
- learn our values—learn to be responsible;
- learn and abide by family/school rules;
- be kind, thoughtful and respectful;
- become a valuable member of society.

One stressful morning, we were almost ready to leave for school when I realised that CJ was covered in grease. He'd been playing with his bike, doing imaginary repairs but with very real tools. Shari had to be at class early for an excursion, and I was going to work straight after drop-off, so I had no choice but to ask CJ to go inside on his own and try to get cleaned up and changed. I told him I'd be back in exactly fifteen minutes.

During the short drive back, I envisioned him blissfully playing Nintendo, with little thought of what he was supposed to be doing, but when I arrived home, he was waiting at the front door. He had his school bag on his back and was cleaned up and ready. Shocked but very pleasantly surprised, I couldn't help saying, "I thought you'd be playing your video game".

He answered simply, "I didn't think I'd be allowed". A chorus of angels sang. He'd never said that to me before. It sounded so 'normal'. Something our family life rarely felt like.

In that short moment, I realised that we weren't losing the battle. Those few words, words that most parents would take for granted, meant hope—hope for a better future. I know it sounds like an everyday moment for most parents, no biggie, but for me, it was a turning point and one of my most memorable days, a day when expectations and reality came together—a day when six little words validated my efforts and renewed my faith in good things to come.

HEALTHY BALANCE

It's important to have that healthy balance when it comes to expectations. If they are too low, children won't learn to cope in the big outside world. If they are too high, a child may give up altogether and become defiant and withdrawn. At a support group meeting, one distraught mum told me that she was frustrated because her ADHD daughter wouldn't practise her writing after school. She had visions of her daughter dropping out of school and would often lose her temper over this issue. Her daughter was five-years-old. She could read basic sentences and had great number skills, but her loving mum felt that she had to push her that little bit further than a regular kid, when in fact she should have praised her daughter for what she was already achieving. It was no surprise that her daughter felt she wasn't good enough, and rather than risk disappointing her mum, she decided to simply not try at all.

We often expect our children to 'measure up to our measure' but there are so many different measures. We all have different interests and ambitions, different strengths and weaknesses. CJ was on the school basketball team, and when he'd arrive home I'd always ask, "Did you score a goal?" A downhearted 'no' was the usual answer, and he often said maybe he shouldn't be on the team because he wasn't scoring goals. When I actually watched him play, I saw that his strength lay in defending and getting the ball from the other team. He was a natural at it, and when I pointed this out to him, his eyes suddenly lit up. He then excitedly said that was what he enjoyed most, and the penny dropped. I realised that getting a goal wasn't the measure as to how well he played. It was in teamwork that he made his mark.

CJ had unknowingly shown me that my measure was, in fact, no measure at all. I'd overlooked what was of real importance. Our perceived expectations (like getting a goal) may be entirely different to what our children can or want to achieve. Make the most of their abilities and what they have to offer. Get to know your child's personal best and have realistic expectations. They can and will improve and achieve.

Expect that they may never be just like you and that is okay too!

TRAVEL TIPS:

- Don't compare with other children (like apples and oranges or puppies and rabbits).
- Adjust your expectations to suit your child's capabilities.
- Have a healthy balance—expect the best but allow for less.

5. THE ANGRY SABOTEUR

"Anger is contagious but so is calm—monitor your thoughts, measure your words, manage your actions to master yourself."

Along the bumpy road of ADHD, our ideals can gradually become lost. With the constant drip, drip (and the occasional torrent) of challenging and often defiant behaviour, our patience is truly tested. We can become people we never wanted to be, disheartened, frustrated and angry.

As a new mum, I began parenting life with excitement, joy, and the best of intentions. I happily looked forward to what the future would bring. The first few baby years were, to a point, what I had expected: not much sleep, dirty nappies, lots of crying, (some from me!) lots of smiles and lots of love. The 'terrible twos' were truly terrible, but again, I thought they were meant to be. By that time CJ's little sister Shari had arrived, so I was looking forward to when CJ would become a more sensible three-year-old. But the 'terrible twos' became the 'terrible threes', and then the 'terrible fours' and 'terrible fives'. I'd heard the word 'no' more times from my pint-sized ball of energy than I think I'd said myself in my entire lifetime. My patience was rapidly diminishing. I became increasingly exasperated with

CJ's constant challenging of my decisions and requests. I grew increasingly impatient with silly behaviours and constant yelling (often mine!) and struggled to keep my anger and resentment at bay.

If you don't find controlling anger to be a problem, I applaud you. Feel free to skip this chapter. Unfortunately, for many parents losing their temper is a regular occurrence. In expressing this excessive anger, we fuel our child's anger. In effect, we sabotage our own efforts toward a happy home life. We lose our temper when we're losing control. Ironically in doing so, it brings the ultimate loss of control, and our credibility slips away.

MOUNTAINS FROM MOLEHILLS

Our biggest dramas sometimes start with the smallest incidents, and by the time we've finished arguing, it's hard to remember what the problem was that started it all. Recognise this and ask yourself 'what is this situation worth?' Don't blow the small things out of proportion.

I remember one time when I lost it with CJ. It was not my proudest moment … I had sent him to clean his teeth before school, but he was taking a long time. I went to check on him and found him making ridiculous faces at himself in the bathroom mirror. "Please clean your teeth," I said. No answer. I repeated the request again, still no answer. I repeated myself again, raising my voice a little. He then looked at me vacantly and began to punch the toothpaste tube with his fist as if that would get the paste onto his brush. I took the tube from him, put the paste onto his brush and handed it to him. He smirked at me, put the wrong end of the toothbrush into his mouth and pretended to smoke it. I could feel my anger building up. I took it out of his mouth and handed it to him again the right way.

"Clean your teeth, or you'll be late for school," I said, clenching my teeth.

"I was!" he yelled back defiantly.

"No, you weren't. C'mon, I'll help you," I said impatiently. I put the brush into his mouth.

He began to scream loudly even though I wasn't hurting him at all. He clenched his teeth and made fists, yelling and struggling. That was it! I'd had enough. I hurriedly brushed over his teeth, not considering that it might be hurting him. At that instant, I didn't care. I was in control again. Suddenly he began to cry, and I realised what I'd done. There was no excuse. I felt ashamed. I'm supposed to be the grown-up. I tried to say sorry, to hug him, but he pulled away. I would have too. Eventually, we made up. I bribed him with a chocolate bar, but the damage was done. I'd succeeded in humiliating him.

He went to school red-eyed, the last thing he needed to start the day off. Neither of us was better off for my actions. I felt guilty all day. I wished I could go to his school, scoop him up and tell him that I really did love him more than anything…

It may seem obvious, but it's vital to recognise when we are becoming angry. How often do we continue on in a stressful situation, knowing that we're becoming angrier by the minute but doing nothing about it until we SNAP! Staying calm in the face of small difficulties makes it easier to face any bigger problems as they arise. There are always alternatives. They don't have to be typical, just what works for you.

Try an entirely different reaction so that your child will stop and take notice. Maybe remind him that the last thing he would like is a visit to the dentist where it might be a drill, not a toothbrush. Use some humour and make light of the situation, keeping him happy while getting the result you want: "Aaah! The decay monsters are in your mouth, quick let's get them!" as you pass him his toothbrush with a quick rib tickle. Of course, this depends on their age. (It probably won't work on a fourteen-year-old!). Taking things a little less seriously can make a huge difference. Laughter and light-heartedness can be the best way to diffuse an annoying situation.

One morning CJ wouldn't put on his shoes. He felt the need to throw them in the air as if trying to juggle them rather than put them on his feet. I reminded him it was a school morning and he needed to wear them. He looked at me sulkily and replied, "You do it". It would have been easy to be angry when he was so disrespectful. Instead, I sat on the floor and tried to put his little shoes on my own much-bigger feet. Confused, he watched as I struggled to get them over my big toe, then he began to smile and soon we were both laughing. In the end, he put them on with a smile, forgetting why he'd not put them on in the first place.

SET THE STANDARD

Of course, it's normal to feel angry during stressful situations, but it doesn't help anyone to act or speak irrationally based on that emotion. If we argue back as a child would, we lower our own standards. If I yelled at CJ, he would yell back, and usually twice as loud. If I tried to grab something from him in frustration, he would hold onto it even tighter, and we would end up in a ridiculous tug-of-war. Our headstrong ADHD children take their cues from our words and actions. After a very emotional, angry episode, they generally won't feel apologetic or remorseful; they'll feel hurt, unloved, and humiliated. Their already low self-esteem will drop even further.

We may feel justified in those few angry moments, but our feelings of guilt and our child's resentment will last much longer than a few moments. If you feel your chest tightening and your patience beginning to falter, stop what you're doing, think about why you are becoming angry and take positive steps to deal with it. Does it have more to do with you than your child? Are you irritated more than normal due to something else? Running late, worried about bills or you just poked yourself in the eye with your mascara? What if it was a different day and you were in a better mood? Let your voice of reason tell your angry self to 'stop and think' then pause for a moment to consider your next action or reaction.

Practise patience. Ask your child what they're thinking and try to understand the reasoning even if you disagree with the actions. Speak with respect. Ask calmly so that you get an honest answer. What was their intent? Were their motives good or bad? If their motives were good, tell them so and explain why their actions have made you angry. Help them to see your point of view. Say, "I am feeling angry because you gave all the milk to the dog and now there is none left for anyone else. It was thoughtful of you to care about Patch, but next time, please ask first."

If their motives weren't good and those angry, irrational thoughts start creeping into your head, take a deep breath and bite your tongue. Think carefully what your reaction should be. Make a conscious decision to choose your words carefully. Ask yourself the following questions

- Are my next words going to help, or humiliate?
- What is the message that I am about to send?
- Is this the message that I really want to send?

When all else fails, ask yourself, "Is this how I would

deal with the situation if someone were watching me?" If the answer is no (and it often is!), then stop and try something else. Take a moment, and then decide what the action is best to take for everybody involved. "If I overreact angrily, he'll feel humiliated, and I'll feel guilty." There are no positives here. So choose not to get angry. Give yourself time to think and tell your child you'll talk with them in a few minutes when you're not so cross. If possible, remove yourself momentarily from the situation. Go to your room and scream into your pillow. Even just go and look at your angry face in the mirror for a bit of a reality check, but whatever you do, give yourself time to think before you react out of anger.

If punishment is necessary, wait until you've calmed down to decide what is appropriate for the situation, and ensure it is a punishment that you can carry out. "You're grounded for a month!" may be what you feel like saying, but in reality, it is virtually impossible to carry out (as well as being unfair).

If it's in the morning, don't bother with, "Right, you can go to bed at 6.30 pm tonight!" A mistake I often made impulsively. They may be great after school, and you won't want to enforce a punishment for something long forgotten.

MOVE ON AND AVOID YOUR TRIGGERS

Once an incident has been resolved and a reprimand or punishment given, consider it over and done with, and *move on*. Start fresh with no resentment toward your child for what has passed, whether you do this five or thirty-five times a day. Don't hold a grudge. Don't sulk. Your child will learn these annoying habits too. One disagreeable incident doesn't have to cloud the whole day.

If it's 'just one of those days' and you feel your frustration growing, take a quick time-out for yourself and find an outlet to reduce your anger. Take a hot shower, go outside for some fresh air, wash some windows or dig in the garden, hang out some washing or do some overdue dusting. Fast and furious was how I usually did it. It's amazing just how much housework you can get done in five minutes without even realising it when you're in angry adrenalin mode.

It's important to know our triggers. When we're aware of them, we can prepare for them or avoid them altogether. Develop an action plan for common problem times before they occur. If your worst time is the morning rush before school, get everything ready the night before. Set your alarm half an hour earlier and have quiet time to yourself before you wake the kids up. Mornings can be nerve-racking even under normal circumstances if you are trying to do a million things at once and to remember just as much.

To master this morning mayhem, the key can be summed up in two words: *be organised!* Your patience (and tolerance!) will then last much longer, and you'll have the necessary time to adjust for bad mornings. If it is on shopping days, devise ways to keep your child busy. Give them a little list of items to collect. Add a little responsibility. "Can you choose us a nice packet of biscuits for after lunch?" They'll feel good that you value their opinion. If it's really a chore, why not take advantage of online shopping. Take comfort that things that bother us today won't bother us this time next year (there'll be new things!) and do what you need to do to make life easier.

If you regularly find yourself in 'angry mode' decide that for the next half hour you won't lose your temper. Then do the same for the following half hour and then the next again. Gradually you'll find that the time in between losing your temper is growing longer and longer if you keep your resolve. This was an approach that I adopted a long time ago. At first, I had usually failed by mid-morning, but I would try harder the next day. Soon the gaps in between became much longer, and I could feel just a bit proud of myself. Now, I find it hard to be too angry about much at all, and when I am, it's become a habit to try and think first.

USE YOUR GUILT WISELY

We've all used anger incorrectly as a release, but this brings only a momentary feeling of power before the guilt sets in. If we've overreacted in anger and feel guilty, we can use this guilt wisely and as a reference to improve our responses in the future, rather than punishing ourselves. When you feel guilty; when you think you should have done something differently or handled a situation in a better way, go with that feeling. Decide what you can do differently in a similar situation next time and even look forward to it (sounds crazy, I know!).

I once said something to CJ in anger and frustration that still haunts me. After yet another angry outburst by him, I told him, "That's it! I'm sending you to *The Naughty Boys Home*!"

Obviously, I knew of no such place, but CJ didn't know that (it may have been a different story if there was!). I picked up the phone and pretended to call. "Hello. Is that the 'Naughty Boys Home'?"

CJ suddenly became frantic, yelling, "No! I'll be good. I promise". In that second, my heart melted, and I was overcome with guilt. I put the phone down and hugged him. I imagine now that he thought he'd be sent to somewhere like Pinocchio's Pleasure Island, the cursed amusement park where bad boys grow ears then tails and turn into donkeys. I vowed never to say something like that so flippantly again. I felt so guilty and have never forgotten it. It might sound like nothing now, but I felt terrible for the longest time.

Of course, we're never going to be completely 'bad temper free'. There will be times when there is no reasoning with a stubborn child or when a raised voice is necessary, but let's start by aiming for better than what we've done in the past. If managing anger has been a problem, aim to improve a little more each day. If we can set a better example by staying calm, the battle is half won. Effectively managing anger brings confidence, improved self-esteem and a happier family life. It's up to you to make that choice.

TRAVEL TIPS:

- Be self-aware. Look ahead to where the road of anger will take you.
- Be prepared to stop, reassess and take the high road.
- Make anger a 'no parking zone' and move on.

6. EMPOWERING YOURSELF

"Don't be the person that makes you feel inadequate."

Parenting is one of the hardest jobs. Parenting a child with ADHD can be twice as difficult if not more. Many of us look for someone to help us to cope with our child, someone that will be able to 'fix' things. We might look to our family doctor, a paediatrician, a psychologist, a school teacher or we might hope that medication will bring a miracle cure. But long ago, after my own quest for help, I realised that the best person to truly help me, the one that will always be there when I think I'm failing—is myself. All the people I've mentioned can be of great assistance, and it's imperative to have those support people around, but they're not on call twenty-four hours a day. There *is* one person that is available to you twenty-four hours a day, and that is you, yourself. Aim to be one of your main supports—aim to be your own best friend. We can be our own worst enemies when it comes to judging and criticising, and in doing so, we are in effect, disabling ourselves.

TAKE BACK CONTROL

Before CJ's diagnosis, one of my main issues was the overwhelming feeling that things were out of my control. I often felt helpless. No matter what I did, the outcome was rarely what I'd hoped for. It was hard arriving at the classroom at the end of the school day, to hear that CJ had to be 'kept in' again. It was hard to know what to say to his teachers, or what possible explanation I could offer. It was hard when CJ came stomping out of the classroom with his little angry face. It was hard to try my best but to always feel inadequate. It was easy to believe I was a second-class citizen, not on a par with all the 'regular' families. Blaming myself was easy. Blaming CJ was easy—all very easy, but all very wrong.

While the diagnosis of ADHD gave us some answers, it didn't help the overall situation straight away. Many people still believed ADHD wasn't real and just an excuse. I would still find myself lamenting, "He should be behaving better. What did I do to deserve this? I must be a bad mother" or simply, "It's not fair". I was thinking with a self-absorbed 'victim mentality'. This wasn't helping me, my son or my family and I came to see that it didn't have to be this way. ADHD didn't *happen* to me. It wasn't some sabotage thrown at me to make my life difficult. It was just *how things were*. It's easy to get stuck on how we think things should be compared to how things actually are. When we can reconcile the two and take the cards we've been dealt, we can move forward. I came to see that I was only looking at things from my view. I wasn't focusing on how this was affecting CJ, and that should have been the primary focus. Ultimately, he would be the one to live his life with the traits of ADHD and the way I dealt with him as a child was going to carry through to his adult life.

It was time to take back control, take the reins of my life, to be stronger and do better for my family. It was time to be grateful for all the good things CJ brought to our family: his energy, his enthusiasm and his beautiful personality (when he wasn't being Mr Grumpy!).

LOOK TO YOURSELF

This transition began with being kinder to myself, ridding myself of any pointless self-pity and instead, empowering myself with knowledge. I had to learn all that I could about ADHD to better understand CJ's personality and to equip myself to help him as best as I could. Like anything else we can feel a bit lost and unsure until we have the right skills, just like starting a new job or driving a car, we need to learn as much as we can about the subject first. I decided to make this my mission and to do it well. I read any books I could find on ADHD. Back in my day, it was the good old library, but fortunately, parents of today have a myriad of options through the internet. With articles, blogs, forums and eBooks, good old Google, Facebook and Instagram, information is a keyword away. I took note of any newspaper or magazine articles, talked to other parents, and joined a support group which focused on helpful strategies. I spoke with the school about ADHD, discussing what I'd learnt with CJ's teachers; and enlisted their help (the proverbial apple on the teacher's desk doesn't go astray!).

I soon came to see that I wasn't helpless, I wasn't a bad mother, my son's challenging behaviour wasn't my fault, or his. The behaviours were a symptom of his struggle to cope with what was expected of him versus what his brain and impulses were telling him to do. I began to see that I did indeed have some power—some influence— and I felt better than I had in a long time. With this newfound self-confidence, I began to change my outlook, actions and demeanour. In doing so, I found that others reacted to me differently. When people think you're a pushover, they will push that bit more. They will comment or criticise freely, but when you're confident and decisive in what you say and do, they will think twice and be more respectful and supportive.

YES, YOU CAN!

Eliminate the word *can't*. Tell yourself that you *can* be a confident, assertive parent, not because I've just said so, but because you really can! It's not like you have to invent the telephone or fly to the moon! (Who would have thought that was possible?) We just have to work on doing what we can with what we have. Even if there's a new issue or drama every day, we can get through these one at a time, using whatever resources we can to help us along the way.

It can be hard getting to this point, so initially if you don't feel confident and empowered, start to change that by acting like you are. That action in itself will help you on the way to feeling more confident; just in the same way that it's hard not to feel happy when we smile.

No one needs to know all the emotions you're feeling at any particular moment, at that parent/teacher interview, at the mums' playgroup. I'm not suggesting hiding all your emotions from everyone or being fake, but acting confidently does make you feel more confident. Put on a smile; remember you're a good person doing a good job. Often, 'regular mums' are quite interested when they realise the difficulties that come with being the parent of an ADHD child and will empathise. It can be hard at first to act confidently when everybody seems to have an opinion, or they offer unsolicited advice, but doing so is a solid stepping stone to help you on the way to empowerment. Act in a friendly but assertive manner, and people are more likely to listen to you and respect what you have to say.

FAKE IT TILL YOU FEEL IT

I was asked to give a talk to secondary school teachers on what it was like to have a child with

ADHD. I felt this was something I should do but, oh, my gosh, to get up and speak to an audience, and an audience of teachers at that! I was scared stiff. I tried to rationalise; they were only people like me, they wouldn't be sitting in the room if they didn't want to listen, it was important to try and help them to understand ADHD children. I knew all of this, but I was still petrified. What if I was stuck for words and went blank? What if I sounded unsure and unconvincing? I realised though that I should take my own advice. I could do this. I spoke to people every day: it's not as if I had to sing it or speak in a foreign language. I was a good parent, right? I was doing my best to help my son. I had a good grasp on ADHD and wanted to help teachers to have a better understanding.

Still, it was unchartered territory for me, but I told myself, "Don't talk the talk if you can't walk the walk". (This seemed more helpful than imagining that everyone in the audience was naked as often suggested!) That decided, I typed up a base speech and wrote it basically how I would say it, highlighting the main points in case I lost my place. This made me feel a bit better, but I was still nervous, so again, I said to myself, "You can do this. You know what you're talking about. Millions of people have spoken in front of an audience. You just need to act confidently," and that was the key. I had to play the part of this confident me. (I'd always fancied myself as an actor so here was my chance!)

The day of the talk came. I was a nervous wreck on the inside, but I didn't let it show. I spoke as if I was confident and before I knew it, I sounded confident in my words and my knowledge. It went surprisingly well. Afterward, some of the teachers asked if I had given talks in many schools as I 'seemed to speak so easily'. (If only they knew the anxious, panicky mess I was beforehand!) I was grateful that I'd managed to portray that amount of confidence, more than enough to get me through, and it had done wonders for my actual self-confidence. I felt empowered and that I could make a difference. It was a great feeling!

NORMAL IS MOSTLY PERCEPTION

If you're at a place right now where you don't feel confident and are often frustrated by your child's not-so-good behaviours, remind yourself that it isn't your fault and self-pity is a luxury we can neither afford nor indulge in. Maybe life doesn't seem normal right now, but we all have our own personal 'normal'.

Learn all that you can about the traits and idiosyncrasies of ADHD. Listen to other people and take in suggestions with an open mind. We're only human; we're not always right.

Don't be afraid to try new ideas and different approaches when it comes to parenting. One of the best things you can do for yourself is to talk to other parents of ADHD children. Problems don't seem as bad when you know there are others in a similar situation; others who understand exactly what you're going through and how you're feeling; others that can share their advice and experiences. Often, you realise that your child is not quite as difficult as you perceive them to be and you can better appreciate their good qualities.

SEEK SUPPORT THAT SUITS

I never thought that I would be part of a support group. I imagined it to be a group of depressed parents, saying, "Woe is me," and looking helpless, but this is far from the truth. At our support group, we had a variety of activities which varied from guest speakers with lively discussions, to a relaxing meditation morning (though I was so relaxed I actually fell asleep!) to just chatting about everyday problems to be tackled. A support group can give you a new circle of friends and a new outlet for your emotions. You can laugh as well as cry occasionally and gain a new perspective on issues. Join a support group either online or in person. If you opt for a group online, ensure it's a positive one and not one where posts are just depressing. Find one that is encouraging and constructive and helps you to feel stronger. If you can't find one that suits you, consider starting your own. Many community houses will have times available for new groups.

You won't ever have everyone's approval, but you don't need it. You can be in control of your life, your actions and emotions even with all the ups and downs. When you're proud of yourself, it doesn't matter who knows, as long as you do. Boost yourself up as you would a friend. Your own genuine self-approval is what counts the most and what will keep you going. Even when you aren't feeling fully self-assured, believe in yourself. Grasp the wheel firmly and confidently with both hands. Act how you *want* to be, and soon this confident attitude will come naturally.

TRAVEL TIPS:

- Empower yourself through knowledge.
- Act confidently until you feel confident.
- Enable yourself by trusting in your own abilities.

7. A POSITIVE PERSPECTIVE

"Seek out the good, and you will discover hidden gems masquerading as ordinary moments, sprinkled throughout each ordinary day."

Now, that we've empowered ourselves, it's important to maintain the feeling and continue to nurture it. That means getting into the habit of positive thinking and keeping things in perspective. This may sound like common sense. It's something we all know, but often we just need a reminder. We all know what we need to do to think more positively, but to put it into daily practice can be hard to keep up. Just like we all know what to eat to stay healthy, but it's easy to get off track and fall into bad habits.

As our thoughts wander throughout the day, we often don't take too much notice. It's just the way we're feeling. We can't help that right? Well, yes, we can. Our minds really do have a mind of their own, and often they betray the self we want to be.

SAY NO TO THE NEGATIVE

In difficult times, it's easy to fall into the trap of negative thinking. The thoughts that we allow inside our heads, and what we tell ourselves about a situation, are our greatest influence. Our thoughts disable us or empower us, make us depressed or make us hopeful depending on our own internal dialogue. If we think positive thoughts, we will act positively, but if we think about gloom and doom, this is how our day will be. We can change that by making a conscious effort to be aware and recognise when negative self-doubting thoughts creep into our heads. To be more aware of these thoughts, sit back as if an observer and pause when you begin to think negatively. Then say to yourself, "Stop" (Out loud works best though you might just look a little bit crazy!) and remind yourself that there's another, more positive way to think.

Now, you might be saying, "Isn't this a book about ADHD? What does this have to do with it?" but we set the atmosphere for our days and for the people around us. When we're calm, focused and positive, this will flow on to our children. We are their main influence and will be for many years, so the first step is getting ourselves into the right headspace. When you become aware of negative and debilitating thoughts, replace them with a positive alternative. Even if you don't believe it straight away, keep it up, act like you believe it and soon you'll be well on the way to the positive thinking habit.

The script might go like this:

Instead of: *Nothing I do seems to work lately, I give up.*

Try: *I'm not having much luck lately, so I'll try a*

new approach.

Instead of: *The teacher wants to see me; what has Jack done now?*

    Try: *I'm grateful to speak to the teacher today so we can work together to solve issues and help Jack.*

Instead of: *Ben's so hyper today; the other mums must think I'm a bad parent.*

    Try: *Ben's so hyper today, the other mums must be grateful he's not their child! (Said to yourself with a smile)*

I had always been a worrier, but worrying was exhausting and being defensive was even more exhausting. I used to think 'that's just me. That it was just how my mind works', but I came to realise (better late than never) that I'm the only person that can choose my thoughts. I'm the only person that can decide which thoughts get validation and which ones get voted out. Just as I could choose to turn off a song on the radio, I could choose to stop worrying about everything; about other people's opinions or about what I hadn't done right. I could stop looking at the negative and look more for the positive, be it a lesson to be learned or a good outcome in whatever situation arose.

Another typical school day and CJ was in trouble again (Yes, really. Sigh…). This time it was for flicking a rubber band and a toothpick in class. While not the crime of the century, the teacher thought it was detention worthy. I did not agree entirely with this, so I spoke to the teacher, Mr Ferris after school. Though uncomfortable on the inside, I tried to convey a confident and chirpy manner. Things were actually going well. Mr Ferris was listening to my view and appeared pleased that I had come in to discuss the situation. That is, it was going well until CJ suddenly entered the conversation with an angry denial of being the instigator of said rubber band—toothpick incident.

He unexpectedly broke into the conversation with the dreaded, "Bullshit," not once, not twice, not three or four times but around seven or eight times at the top of his voice. And there I was, defender of my precious son, now totally embarrassed in front of this serious, sensible (and quite cute) vice-principal. In an instant, CJ and I had lost all credibility in our defence. Then, to top it off, I felt tears welling in my eyes; no please, not tears, not now. I managed to get out a mumbled, "Sorry," and we left as quickly as possible.

I must admit I was furious. More than furious; I was almost maniacal. I glared at CJ. "How could you do that? You weren't even in trouble from me about the stupid rubber band thing!" As I drove home, I considered all options—dye my hair, change my name by deed poll, wear dark glasses and a moustache around Mr Ferris, change schools, change countries, maybe even continents…

Finally, at home CJ was in his room grounded for all eternity (and yes, I tell you not to do that!). I sat down and cried, all the while thinking 'sorry for myself' thoughts. After a few minutes of this feeling-sorry-for-myself state, and no white knight arriving on a majestic horse to save me, it occurred to me that this was not the end of the world (it would have been nice at this point, but a little too easy).

FIND THE POSITIVE

Okay, I thought, what's done is done, and while totally humiliating to me, it was probably just another day with a pain-in-the-bum-kid for the teacher. He may even have found it amusing. Well, maybe I wouldn't go quite that far, but what could I do to make this situation better? How could anything positive come from today?

After a few minutes deliberation, I went into CJ's room. He was upset. I think he even surprised himself with his outburst. "Honey," I said, "there is no doubt about it, you are in trouble, but it isn't the end of the world". He looked a little relieved. I continued on. "I'm really disappointed in you for swearing at your teacher, but there is something you can do to make this better." A glimmer of hope appeared in his tired little eyes. "There are two choices. You can go to school tomorrow, say nothing to Mr Ferris and you will forever avoid him and feel embarrassed when you see him, or you can be mature and go straight to his office in the morning, apologise for your bad language and the matter will finish there and then. You can show him that you really are a good kid and you just had a bad moment."

Of course, at first, he didn't want to do either, but he eventually realised what was in it for him if he did the right thing; and thankfully, that's exactly what he did. He came home from school at least a little proud of himself, a world away from the day before. I spoke to Mr Ferris who said that they'd had a 'talk', and things were fine (as fine as they could be for now anyway). I thanked him, and that was the end of it.

If I'd let my negative thoughts take over, I would have spent a lot more time being angry and worrying about the situation. Instead, something positive was able to come from something negative. Thinking differently about the situation gave me a different perspective and in turn, a different result (I didn't have to move to Africa!).

Looking for the good in the bad is a great habit to adopt even though it can seem as if we're looking for a white button in a blizzard. If we look hard enough, it might just appear when we least expect it. Sure, we can feel a little sorry for ourselves at times, but we don't have to let these feelings take control. We can decide which perspective we will have on things.

Not long ago my now grown daughter Shari called me, despondent about her day. On her way to university that morning, she had been stopped at traffic lights when a car hit her from behind. This caused her car to be propelled forward, colliding with the vehicle in front. The drivers swapped information, and though shaken, Shari was unhurt and still able to drive her car. She arrived at class but was having trouble getting an important assignment submitted due to a technical issue, and time was running out. Just what she didn't need! There was not much I could do but offer moral support and kind words.

As expected, she arrived home lamenting, "What an awful day that was!" Then suddenly as if a light bulb went off, her mood changed. "No wait," she said. "It was actually a great day. I had a car crash, but no one was hurt, I could still drive to uni, I ended up getting my assignment in on time—so yes, it was a great day!"

What a perfect example of positive thinking. She could have remained downcast. "Oh, why did that happen to me? Now, I have to book my car in to get fixed and, oh, how stressful trying to get that assignment in." But she took the positives from her day and let those shine through (Mum was very proud!).

It can be hard to keep a positive perspective when your child is misbehaving, and it feels like whatever you say goes in one ear out the other, but keep up the positive-thinking habit, and it will definitely pay off. It's hard to imagine this when some days it can feel like we're living in an episode of a bad sitcom.

At first, like me, you may have to talk yourself into being this more positive self. Think good thoughts 'Tomorrow is a new day, I'm a good parent, and I'm doing the best I know how. Tell yourself 'It's okay, nobody died, and the house didn't burn down' (unless, of course, it did!). Take care of yourself and your thoughts as you would take care of a loved one or a friend.

You wouldn't put down a friend who deals with the challenges that you encounter. You would remind them of all the good they do and of the good in their child. So, do the same for yourself.

HUMOUR TO THE RESCUE

Life with our ADHD children or any child for that matter will be full of highs and lows but we can take things as they come with a calm and positive outlook and by utilising that wonderful gift called humour. We can use humour to retain our inner peace when we look for the lighter side in a situation. It's is one of our most valuable tools to keep us on the positive track. It doesn't even matter what we find funny, but just that we get that fun feeling. Laughing just makes us feel good. It's good for you and good for everyone else. How often have we laughed when thinking back on what seemed very serious at the time?

CJ was supposed to be cleaning his room (yes, the dreaded messy room), but was making no attempt. After being patient and getting nowhere, I finally reprimanded him. He looked at me with an irritated huffy scowl on his face and yelled. "I'm not doing it! I want to leave here forever!" I knew that his words were designed to make an impact, because he thought it would upset me, but also out of frustration, so instead of getting angry with him, I did something else. I put the same huffy scowl on my face and said to him. "Okay, I don't want to do the dishes, so I think I'll leave here forever". Then, "I don't want to do the washing, so I think I'll leave here forever".

I rattled off a list of all the things that I didn't want to do right down to brushing my teeth and picking my nose until we were both laughing. "C'mon, pal," I said, "let's get this room sorted out," and with the mood changed for the better (plus a little organisational help from mum), that's exactly happened.

We all tend to worry too much about small incidents that should be dealt with and forgotten. Often, what we think is a huge incident is really nothing in the great scheme of our lives. We don't have a lot of years in which to teach our children and set them on the right path. This time goes fast, and the way we deal with frustrations and issues will set the scene for their adult years.

Our kids are bound to get into quarrels and conflicts with other children at some point. Most of these sort themselves out due to the resilience of children and their ability to put things behind them. It becomes more difficult when these quarrels cause conflict situations with other parents, especially if they are not the most understanding. If we're lucky we will escape relatively unscathed from the wrath of other parents, but it's good to be prepared for a hostile confrontation should one arise.

THE PARENTAL FIRING-RANGE

There will always be *that parent* who feels the need to put on a big show in defence of their child when they believe that your child is at fault in an incident. They might be angry and irrational, an emotional volcano erupting in front of you, verbally attacking you and your beloved offspring. Your spontaneous reaction might be to fire back in retaliation. "Excuse me! How dare you! Now, just wait a minute!" and you yourself become a matching eruption.

Alternatively, you might be so upset that you immediately yell at our own child. "What have you done now? Can't you just behave yourself?" (Just writing that made me feel stressed so imagine how it would feel in person!). Fortunately, there's a better and healthier way in the form of calm, controlled communication. Even if the other parent is neither calm nor controlled, we can always be the one who steers the situation. It takes two people to escalate an argument, but just one sensible person to de-escalate it. This may already be how you handle things, and if so that's fantastic, but sometimes we can be caught off guard so forewarned is forearmed.

LET THE OTHER PARENT FINISH WHAT THEY'RE SAYING.

When you don't argue back, they might trail off and possibly feel a bit silly. Say nothing for a few seconds to restore some calm. Calmly repeat what you heard to be the problem, so the other parent feels heard. Some people just have to vent and are satisfied to be heard. Don't take it personally; just be glad that you're not the angry one.

DON'T IMMEDIATELY DEFEND OR BLAME YOUR CHILD.

Other children can be good liars, and our kids make good scapegoats. Hold your emotions and thank the parent for coming to you. Apologise that there has been an issue (not for anything else unless you know for certain) and tell them you'll discuss it with your child. This is often enough.

ONCE AWAY FROM THE SITUATION.

Ask for your child's account. Let your child know that it's okay to tell you the truth (their version at least) to open the way for discussion. Decide if any further action needs to be taken when you're calm and have a clear head. It's upsetting to have any sort of confrontation especially if you're just holding things together. If need be, go and have a quick cry in your room or punch a pillow, or just put the incident behind you, your pride intact, ready to move forward.

FIND YOUR INNER CALM

Take comfort that today's issues won't last forever. Ask yourself if you'll be worrying about this one year from now. Issues that are a problem this year will usually have disappeared by next year. Ask yourself what's the worst thing that can happen. Once we accept the worst, we can only go up from there and hope to improve on that. Asking yourself these questions is a great way to keep things in perspective. These were strategies that Dale Carnegie encouraged in his book *How to Stop Worrying and Start Living* many years ago, and they're still valid today. This book was a great influence on my own life even before I had CJ. Fun fact—when I bought that book, I was worried about what people would think if they knew I'd bought it! By the time I'd finished reading it, I no longer cared.

Another great way to keep positive is by utilising quotes and mantras. They may be cliché, but they've stood the test of time because they're effective and true, generally with a lesson to be learnt or some wisdom to pass on. Sites such as Instagram have an abundance of wonderful words and quotes. Find those that inspire and uplift you and have them where you can see them each day. Set them as a desktop background or incorporate them into your living space. Below are a few that I try to live by. I often get off track and have to remind myself, but I always go back to them:

'Life is too short to be little' by Benjamin Disraeli. Don't allow insignificant worries to take over your life. Remember what's really important

'Every day is a new life to a wise man' by Dale Carnegie. Start fresh each day, forget the troubles of yesterday and look to this new day with hope and optimism.

Make up your own daily mantra or affirmation or find some that set the mood for your day. It could be something as simple as 'I am a good parent, doing a good job and today will be a good day'. I created the one below, and it works perfectly for me:

Appreciate today, for this ordinary day with its minor annoyances and over-thought worries is the day you would pray to go back to, should tragedy strike tomorrow.

Whenever I'm feeling down, sorry for myself, or unappreciative, I recall these words and immediately return to a more positive mindset.

If sayings and quotes aren't your thing, find what works for you to keep up the positive perspective. Look to the internet for inspirational, motivational speakers to listen to. YouTube is a great place to start, and it's free. Find what suits you: you don't need a lot of time, you can even listen while you do dishes or exercise. The right speaker can boost you up and make you feel like you can conquer anything. They can put you in a positive frame of mind, ready for any challenge.

As Forest Gump said, "Life is like a box of chocolates, you never know what you're gonna get". There's often some chocolates that we don't like in amongst the delicious ones, so what do we do? Do we throw away the whole box? No, we just take them as they come. We may find a use for the ones we don't like. We might share them with the kids, or we may eventually develop a taste for them. We don't expect 100% perfection. When we don't get perfect kids, or we don't act like perfect parents, let's put these moments where they belong and into perspective, as just a small part of the package that is our life—and go on to enjoy the rest of it.

TRAVEL TIPS:

- Stop negative thoughts in their tracks—be self-aware.
- Look for the good in any situation—make it a challenge
- Start each daily journey in the right gear—P for positive!

8. YOUR SELF-ESTEEM

*"The most valuable approval you can have is your own—
and be sure to write a list!"*

Self-esteem—the regard in which we hold ourselves;
the confidence we have in our own abilities. It
sounds simple enough to believe in ourselves, so why
are we so often our own worst critics? Why also do
we place so much importance on the beliefs and
opinions of other people? Why are we so hard on
ourselves?

I always wanted everything to be 'just right'. If
visitors were expected, then the house had to look
perfect. If I was making a birthday cake, it had to be
extremely elaborate, and I could stay up till three am
to get it just right. Often, I wouldn't finish things
because I couldn't seem to get them perfect, but in
setting such high targets for myself, I was setting
myself up for failure.

Nothing is ever perfect. Perfection is merely an
opinion, and to the self-critical nothing is ever good
enough.

APPRECIATE 'SELF'

If you're doing your best and are proud of your
efforts, that's fantastic. That is how it should be, but

for many of us, including my 'young-mum self' coping with a hyperactive child, I rarely felt I could be proud of myself. I wrestled with feelings of inadequacy. I questioned my own decision making and always second guessed myself. I never felt that my best was good enough. If I could go back in time, I would tell that 'young-mum self' to hold her head up high and to keep doing what she's doing. I'd tell her to ask for help when she needed it, but most of all, that her best was good enough. And that is what I will tell you today.

As parents of ADHD children, our best efforts can never seem enough and results are not always what we had hoped for or envisioned. We begin to question if we even know what we're doing. We start to see things in ourselves that we dislike; losing our temper, becoming overly anxious or just feeling lost. We begin to feel like people we never intended to be, and gradually this eats away at our confidence and self-esteem. For a long time that was me, guilty of all the above. Thinking back: generally, I was a people pleaser. I didn't like to say no. I worried if I let someone down by a decision I'd made or something I'd said. I wasted energy by worrying about pretty much everything and the universe in general. Not necessarily all the time but too much of the time.

Many of us with self-esteem issues are chronic worriers, but unless we're looking for solutions, worrying just makes us feel bad. It can't change anything. When we procrastinate or make decisions that don't sit well with us, we feel bad. But when we 'do good', we 'feel good'. We're happiest when we live to our ideals with honesty and integrity and when we are the person we want to be. To not live this way is a burden. It's easy to put on that happy face, but ultimately, it's on the inside that we need to feel good about ourselves.

There came a time that I knew changes had to be made to reclaim my shrinking self-esteem before my self-doubt devoured it completely. These weren't massive changes. I didn't have a gambling habit or drink a bottle of whisky a day. I didn't need to move states or change my name. It was just small changes that would make a difference. If we look to others for our self-esteem, we'll never be truly happy. We won't ever please everyone, so the best place to start is with ourselves. At first, it may seem like daunting task.

MAKE A LIST

Sometimes we don't even know why we don't feel good. It's usually a combination of things. I found the best way to start was with a list. I made my first list of 'things I don't like about me' many years ago when I decided to make some much-needed changes. I didn't like that:
- I would never say 'no' to anyone;
- I didn't know how to be assertive;
- I was always in a hurry and disorganised;

- I never did what I really wanted to do;
- I felt inferior because of CJ's seemingly naughty behaviour;
- I would often lose my temper with him;
- I wasn't enjoying time with my new baby son;
- I wasn't spending enough time with my daughter;
- I always had a pile of laundry to be folded, sitting on the lounge room couch. (A small one but it annoyed me to no end!)

It's funny how those small things like to eat away at us, like termites, picking away from the inside at our foundations. Before we know it we're falling apart. One by one I gradually changed the things on my list, and most importantly I learned that much of it was only in my own mind; much of it was my choice, and all of it was my own doing, and well-within my power to change.

I love lists. Lists organise our thoughts. They give us clarity and a starting point. As we mark things off as done, we get that feel-good kick. Start your own list right now with anything you'd like to change. They don't have to be big things, just things that matter to you.

START SMALL

The smallest of changes can give us the biggest results. Small goals reached result in a happy self and add to our feelings of self-satisfaction. You might surprise yourself with what you put on your list and how easy it is to alter bad patterns and negative thinking. Even the small annoyances can go on your list. It might look something like this:

- I don't say what I really mean;
- I need to exercise more;
- I don't laugh enough;
- I am always hard on myself;
- I need to make more time for myself;
- I eat too many potato chips (I'm still trying to conquer that one!)

This isn't a list you have to show anyone so you can be totally honest with yourself. One by one work your way through, ticking off as you go, changing bad habits or replacing them with good ones. One that is especially important on the above list is making some time just for you. We all need some 'me time' and if we don't make it a priority, no one else will either.

LEARN TO SAY NO WITHOUT GUILT

It's important not to over-commit yourself and your time. We can't always be rushing. You don't have to be superwoman and supermum as well. Learn to say no. Often, there is just too much to do and not enough time in the day. There may be work, then shopping, then you become 'mums' taxi' taking one child to basketball and one to gymnastics, then meals to cook and housework to be done. There might be reading at school, as well as looking after a baby, coping with your ADHD child's needs as well as those of your partner. Maybe you're minding another child, there's a school council meeting (because you thought you should join), then that Tupperware party and the list goes on...exhausting!

So, maybe you will just have to say, "No, I'm sorry, I won't be able to this time" to volunteering at the school cake stall, or to accepting an extra shift at work, or to going somewhere that you really don't want to go—perhaps the Tupperware party!

Decide what's important and what you can leave out. Prioritise your time. Don't beat yourself up that you couldn't do something. Stick to your decision, knowing it was made for the good of you and your family. When we're under pressure, we are more prone to lose our patience and become frazzled and angry which doesn't help the behaviour of our children.

PLAN AHEAD

A really simple way to raise our spirits and feel good about ourselves is to plan our time. It's difficult to stay calm and in control if you are trying to blow dry your hair, feed the baby, look for school clothes, make lunches, do last night's dishes and successfully cope with your ADHD child. Sounds more like chaos! If you're running around in hyper mode, how is your ADHD child supposed to learn how to exit hyper mode?

If something needs doing and won't take longer than five minutes just do it straight away. I am a huge procrastinator, so this five-minute rule really helped me. I would often bring in the washing and throw it on the couch to be folded, but it could sit there for a day or two (okay, maybe all week!). I'd look at it feeling guilty that I hadn't done it. This feeling would hang over my head like a dark cloud, making me feel bad when it would have only taken a few minutes of my time each day to eliminate both the bad feeling and the folding!

Write a list (yes another!) and plan ahead for the next day. With anything that needs to be done or prepared. Even decide on your clothes for the next day. You won't be stressed and impatient if half the work has already been done. This might seem unrelated to your self-esteem but it all ties in with feeling good, feeling productive and feeling in control. All of which are part of the parcel that boosts our self-confidence.

TOP UP THE TANK

It's important to top up your personal fuel-tank with some form of relaxation on a regular basis. Relaxation doesn't have to mean you should join a yoga class or learn to meditate, but we all need something to stay in tune with ourselves—something that helps us to feel refreshed. In doing activities that we enjoy, we close our minds to the problems that life brings us, even just for a little while.

Plan it into your day. Make it a habit. Maybe reading a book or magazine or just being out in the fresh air gardening. It might be listening to music, doing a hobby that you enjoy, getting a weekly massage, visiting an old friend, painting a picture, or reading a book.

Then again it might be something more energetic like rock-climbing or kayaking. Exercise might be your relaxation. A twenty-minute walk along the beach or walking your dog can be relaxing as well as beneficial. We all know exercise and being out in the fresh air boosts our feeling of wellbeing, so incorporate that into your day if you don't already.

Simply put—*care for yourself.* It's important to take a time-out from being 'just mum' (or dad) and the rollercoaster of ADHD. Just to be you. Just to feel calm and relaxed. We wouldn't let our car run out of fuel. We wouldn't ignore checking the oil and water levels— if we did, we might face the consequences of a broken-down car. So don't try to run on empty. Keep a regular check on yourself and avoid a potential breakdown.

NOTHING TO HIDE

Another aspect that can deplete our self-esteem is the communications and interactions we have with others, especially other parents. In those early years, I felt isolated and not part of the normal group. I kept to myself. The problem with that is we don't live in a solitary world, and we need to interact with a variety of other people, not just for school, work or business, but also to feel a sense of belonging. Today's world, fortunately, is very accommodating. There is a vast range of options through the internet to communicate with other parents in similar situations. This can be a lifeline and great way to share ideas, to gain feedback and validation, and also provide that important sense of belonging.

That said, we still need our day-to-day interactions with others. This can feel very different face-to-face and if you tend to keep to yourself, it can be hard to alter that pattern. Before the diagnosis of ADHD, I felt that I had to always apologise for my son's unpredictable behaviour. I wrongly blamed CJ as well as myself. As a parent, I felt I was inferior. Fast-forward to the diagnosis and the resulting realisation that I had been a good (albeit naïve) mother: my perception of myself changed for the better. My newfound confidence began to shine through; other people warmed to that and new friendships were formed.

I once read somewhere that most people like you as much as you like them, and when I think about this it really seems true. People are usually as interested in you as you are in them, so ask others about themselves. Listen to their woes even when you have our own. Even though their issues may be vastly different to ours, they still hold the same amount of anxiety and worry, and we realise we're not all so different after all.

TO TELL OR NOT TO TELL—THAT IS THE QUESTION!

ADHD doesn't have to be the all-consuming factor in your conversations. You don't have to tell everyone you meet that your child has ADHD. Depending on the situation, they can fit in like any other child. It's not a secret, it's nothing to be ashamed of, but mentally it's good to remove the subject of ADHD from some of your interactions and conversations and allow the focus to be on other topics. Disclosure can just be on a need to know basis, such as with those spending a lot of time with your child: family, teachers, good friends, parents of your child's good friends. Though sometimes non-disclosure can backfire when you least expect it!

CJ had decided he wanted to learn guitar. Always happy for him to try something new, I enrolled him in a small after-school class that had only three students. I thought this would be ideal, by comparison to a large group. I was happy to sit outside for the hour and let him get on with it. As he was so motivated and enthusiastic, I didn't feel the need to tell the guitar teacher about CJ's ADHD. This was going fine until the third lesson when the teacher informed his students that they would be finishing ten minutes earlier than normal. The other children came happily out of the class, but CJ was still in the music room. I could hear his voice, but I had no idea what was going on, so I went in and found CJ having quite a vocal debate with Mr Guitar Teacher. He argued that because they were finishing ten minutes earlier, the teacher should give him back at least a dollar.

"It was $10 for an hour not $10 for fifty minutes." CJ protested, and with his staunch sense of what was fair and what wasn't, he was demanding a dollar back or an extra ten minutes next lesson. (to be honest, he did have a point!). I calmed CJ down and explained that it was okay. It was my $10, and as it was a one-off, we would let it go. The guitar teacher looked a little perplexed by an eight-year-old challenging him on the payment, so I thought I'd better let him know that CJ did have ADHD and that what CJ thought, he generally said out loud where others wouldn't. No harm was done, though I probably should have mentioned it initially. Oops!

FAMILY FOIBLES

Relatives and those close to us can be a mixed bunch. Some may have understanding, empathy and want to help. Some grandparents, like CJ's fortunately, may think your child is just the bees-knees and see no problem at all. Enjoy this! Others may be disinterested, passing ADHD off as a 'fad'. Some may criticise you and your parenting, adding that stronger discipline is what's needed. Don't allow relatives to destroy your confidence by questioning you or your parenting strategies, in turn making you question yourself. Believe in yourself and do what works for you.

Explain to relatives and those close to you about ADHD in simple terms or give them some basic reading material. Most of all, be confident in yourself. When they see that you're in control, they'll be less likely to question or criticise. Do accept constructive criticism and thank people for well-meaning advice. Tell them you'll keep it in mind and just go about things in your own way. They're usually only trying to help even though it's not how it may seem at the time.

If visiting certain people becomes more stressful than worthwhile, stop punishing yourself and your child. If you've tried your best to help others understand and they still refuse to accept this 'ADHD nonsense' then fine, so be it, and don't lose any sleep over it. Limit visits to just short ones or simply stop taking your child to visit until you feel the time is right. There doesn't have to be any family feud over this. It doesn't need to be said. Just quietly, gradually change your visiting habits. Your child is your priority, and you can still visit on your own with no harm done to the relationship.

Social media or social mania?

Social media has a lot to answer for when it comes to our feelings of self-worth. We're constantly bombarded with happy pictures: party fun, fabulous outings, happy children, a brand-new car, a beach holiday, sexy selfies, romantic date nights and the list goes on. I'm not saying that's a bad thing generally. Most of us are happy to share in our family and friends' happiness. If there's no issue, it can be a positive thing.

Problems arise though when we have low self-esteem, coupled with an often-erratic household, because then we begin to compare. We look at what we don't have, and it doesn't seem fair. Then we get down—down about not being one of the 'happy people' and down about life in general. We see how stunning Becky looks in readiness for a child-free night out as she poses, phone in hand. And here we are, sitting in sweatpants at eleven pm on a Saturday night, our insomniac ADHD child finally asleep, an almost empty glass of Shiraz in hand, munching through a tube of Pringles, and watching a repeat of Love Actually. Ughhh!

Keep in mind that behind the happy-photo-smiles, there are many sad faces too, just unseen. All people have their own worries and issues, good days and bad days. They're just not posting their bad day pics, so don't place too much emphasis on what you see. Happy facades don't always tell the whole story.

Of course, it can go both ways. You might be a regular poster on social media and appreciate the online company and validation that you get from comments and likes, etc. If not, and if looking at endless social media posts just makes you feel dejected, then spend less time looking. If you feel pressure when you're online that you're 'not as good' or 'not as interesting' or that maybe you haven't 'liked' enough posts or made any witty comments, it's more a hindrance to your life so put a stop to it. If you can, get rid of it all together.

If you want to stay in the loop just check in occasionally. Tell close friends you won't be online as much and take the pressure off. You don't have to say why unless you want to, or simply say it was becoming too much of a distraction. Take it off your phone and just log in on your lunch break or after dinner. You won't miss out. You don't need all those instant snaps and notifications impacting your day. You'll be surprised how much better you feel when you free up that space in your mind and fill it with your own unique, happy things.

YET ANOTHER LIST

Now, I want you to make a final list (sorry!). This time, look at the good in your life more than the bad. We all have positives in our lives, but too often we take them for granted. Again, it can be anything that makes you feel proud. It's just for you.

You might have something like:
- I help my friends; I am honest and caring;
- I give my children a loving home;
- I have an awesome sense of humour;
- I did a good job with the fancy dress costume;
- I help in the football canteen;
- My cat thinks I'm the best person in the world;
- I have written my lists and not just skimmed through this chapter! ☺

If you know that you're doing your best with a good heart and good intentions, let that be your validation. If you feel you've made a wrong decision, say to yourself 'okay, that didn't work out, but I will learn from this and do better next time'. Your penalty is then, to store the experience safely away for future reference, and to place any negative feelings toward yourself in the 'throwaway basket' of your mind and *move on*.

Really good people can have really bad self-esteem when they try to please everyone, everyone that is, except themselves. Misguidedly they place themselves at the bottom of the importance list. If that sounds like you, move yourself closer to the top of the list. The top position is ever-changing and depends on the day. Ensure you're up there when you need to be. Be kind to yourself and make yourself a priority.

As Eleanor Roosevelt said, "No one can make

you feel inferior without your consent". We allow this to happen. We allow ourselves to be judged by others and who's to say those judges are even qualified. Just as you can choose to criticise or condemn yourself, you can also choose to give yourself a pat on the back. Be aware of your feelings and apply a positive thinking habit. When that pesky inner voice tries to tell you that you're not good enough or you've done the wrong thing, tell it to belt up! Replace self-critical talk with positive affirmations. Appreciate your good qualities. Aim for your own personal best and be confidently happy with that.

TRAVEL TIPS:

- Learn to say no or be prepared to crash.
- Keep your personal fuel tank topped up.
- Value the opinion that matters the most—your own.

9. COMPLIANCE USING MOTIVATION

"Doing because they choose to, beats doing because they have to."

It's not always the big issues that are our main problems, but the small day-to-day frustrations that can test us the most. One of the hardest tasks we can face is getting our children to readily comply with often simple requests.

At an ADHD Support Group meeting, one mum commented that her son rarely listened to what she said and never did any jobs at all, not even tidy his own room. Heads started nodding, and most of the other mums agreed. Now, while never totally enthusiastic, CJ did do chores at home. I told this to the group, and the same woman asked how I *made him* help at home. I knew that I used various techniques and gave some vague examples, but I couldn't find exactly the right words to get my point across. It was only later at home that it occurred to me—one word would have explained it perfectly, and that word was *motivation*.

MOTIVATION MAGIC

CJ's ADHD seemed to be more of a motivation

deficit at times than an attention deficit. I saw this by how much energy he would put into an activity that he was interested in and sustain concentration for a long period of time. If he was building Lego models or playing a computer game, he could become totally immersed. When it came to something that he had little interest in, he would 'forget' and had to be reminded of what he was supposed to be doing, such as cleaning his room or doing his homework.

You're probably saying most kids will do this, but the main difference is that non-ADHD children generally know why they should be doing a task even if they get side-tracked. Our ADHD children can't see the point of most of our requests. They see no obvious reason to comply, so the key to getting our kids to do what *we want* is to make *them want* to do it for themselves.

NATURAL REWARDS

A great way to encourage our children to comply with our requests is to plant the motivation— to give them the incentive. That doesn't mean that a child must get a reward for everything that we ask them to do. Motivation shouldn't be confused with bribery, but it does mean that we can point out the distinct advantages that will come with doing what we ask of them.

Everything we do is for a reason. I found by incorporating the benefits of a task into my requests,

CJ would see for himself, the advantage in complying. Some parents might say, "Why should I? They should just do as they're told". But the answer is simple. It removes the stress of trying to force a defiant child to comply. This, in turn, saves us time, (maybe some of our sanity as well!) and encourages a more positive relationship.

We all use rewards or consequences to motivate ourselves, even if it's subconscious. There's always a reason that we do the things we have to do, no matter how mundane or unpleasant the task. Why do we wash our dishes? We might say 'because we have to', but there is always another reason, a motive, even if we don't consciously think about it. Obvious reasons could be that we will have clean dishes for next time or so that the kitchen will look tidy. It might be so that we can relax afterward and watch a movie without having to get up again, or just because it makes us feel good when they're out of the way. These are the natural rewards that come with doing this task. Our ADHD kids can't always see this end result, so we need to make the possible advantages clear for them, point out what the rewards are—what's in it for them.

It may sound as if I am encouraging selfishness, but we have the foresight that our ADHD children do not. They don't think ahead—"Oh, if I do this then I can do that". They only think of *now*, so it's important to encourage an awareness of the value in doing tasks by helping them to think ahead. Ask your child how they might benefit from doing a particular task and let him work out the possible rewards for himself. You might have to give hints at first!

If you get this homework done now what will happen?

> *I will have the rest of the night free to relax.*
> *I will have time to play my video game before tea.*
> *You and dad will be proud of me.*

When your bedroom is tidied, what might happen?

> *It will be easier to find my toys.*
> *There'll be more room to set up the car track.*
> *A friend can come over to play.*

The dreaded messy room can be a continual source of dispute. Don't be a frustrated, broken record. For the seventeenth time, you demand that your child cleans their room or else. Or else what? I never really had that answer. Telling a naturally disorganised, distractible child to just 'clean your room' can be like asking a squirrel to tidy up your backyard. They might spot a few things to grab here and there, but for the most part, they would flit from one spot to another, soon getting bored, not finding any nuts (incentive) and giving up.

To our ADHD children cleaning their room can seem overwhelming, but it doesn't have to be.

Instead of making it a challenge, make it challenging. "Let's see how much you can get done in fifteen minutes. That sounds manageable, right?" Explain that if they leave it all week, it will waste at least two hours of their weekend cleaning up (or possibly all day!) and nightly speedy clean-ups are more manageable and less stressful.

ORGANISATIONAL AIDS

Ensure a child has some type of organisation tools, tubs, boxes and shelves for specific items (and especially an in-room rubbish bin!). Divide things into smaller parts. Give them specific instructions— "Put the Lego into the bucket/ the books onto the bookshelf'. Check. Praise. Have a break. Start again. "Put your clothes in the basket and the rubbish into the bin." It helps to use a bit of camaraderie. "If you pass me the rubbish bin, I'll empty it out for you," or "Collect your clothes and I'll take them to the laundry for you". You may have to be that initial influence, but it's well worth the effort. Your child will feel good about what they've achieved. You can point out how nice it is to play in a tidy room and tell them to remember this feeling for next time.

We incorporated a tidy room into the pocket money. Aside from their regular jobs, they had to at the least, have a tidy room by pocket money day, if not, then no pocket money. It sounds harsh, but it worked. It didn't have to be spotless, and they still did their fifteen-minute tidy each night. If their room isn't up to your standard, but they've tried to do a good job, don't get worked up over it, just appreciate their effort then shut the door.

It's also a great idea to have your child make their own lists to help keep them on track. It might be which toys go in which tubs, what they need to take to school, activities they have on during the week, or just things they need to remember, such as their daily tasks at home.

CHOOSE CHORES

Household chores are a necessary part of a child's routine. Our children can be motivated to help and to form good habits. Eventually, they will expect *to be expected* to help. Sometimes it's easier to do things ourselves, but we pay for it later with lazy teenagers. Let them choose their jobs from a list. This tells them that helping at home is 'a given', but they can have some control over their input. We had a minimum number per week to be done.

Make up a chart for them to tick so that they can see what they have achieved and know who's doing what (yes, I love charts as much as I love lists!). Alternate the jobs, so the boys aren't always the ones bringing in the bins or the girls folding the washing. It makes it easier when they know whose turn it is to dry the dishes or feed the dog, therefore, fewer arguments about the fairness of things. It helps to do chores together as a team effort. Schedule a time and put on some catchy music and sing or bop along as you do the dishes together.

Most of all let them know that they are a valuable part of the family and that their help is appreciated. When a task has been completed, even just because of the motivation you've given, praise your child and reiterate the advantages you pointed out, so they can *feel* them. "Well done, you've finished. Look at all this extra space in your room. Go and mark it off your job sheet. Great, now you can go out and play. Let's watch that TV show together now," etc. Their self-esteem will be boosted, and they'll have that great feeling of accomplishment.

SPECIFIC REWARDS

More specific rewards can be used wisely and in moderation. There will be times that we want our child to do something that they find difficult or uncomfortable. CJ was to be in the school concert as was every other child in the school, but he was most adamant that he did not want to participate in it. I could tell he was embarrassed about singing and dancing in front of an audience, but it was part of the school program and much class time was spent on it.

I tried to point out the advantages: it would be fun, it would be a good experience, and Dad would be coming to watch—but to no avail. So, I made him an offer. "CJ, I know you really don't want to do this, but I really want you to, so if you do this for me, I will do something for you. The concert will go for about an hour so you can have me for an hour on another day, and we'll do whatever you like, play footy, go on a bike ride, build some Lego or do some cooking." CJ thought that this was a great idea and chose the Lego option. Though not super-keen, he participated in the concert with minimal objection. The funny thing was that afterward, he told me he'd enjoyed the concert and laughed that I was rewarding him for having a good time, but that was fine by me. My mission was complete. (And I enjoyed our Lego time!)

Rewards should be suitable for the situation and can be as simple as having the light on at bedtime for an extra fifteen minutes or reading an extra bedtime story. The reward can be low cost or preferably no cost. If you find that a reward that once motivated your child is no longer effective, don't increase the size of the reward—just change the reward to something different.

USING REQUEST REVERSAL

When our children want something, it's a good opportunity to subtly use their request as a motivation to get them to do something that we want. In doing this, we reverse their request to suit our needs and place some responsibility for the outcome with our child.

One Friday night Bob arrived home from work and found eleven-year-old CJ and four-year-old Harry sitting in the lounge folding a large pile of washing together. The boys were folding enthusiastically and checking with me that they were doing a good job. There was no forcing them to do this, and they seemed happy to be helping. Their dad was so surprised at this sight that he assumed he was in the wrong house. But no, not quite, just one short conversation achieved this.

The script went like this:

CJ: "Mum, can we stay up late and watch the footy game tonight?"

Me: "Well, I hadn't really planned on a late night (actually I had), but if you two will help me out with the folding, we could stay up a bit later."

CJ (looking hopeful): "And we could watch the footy too?"

Me: "Sure we can, sounds good."

That was all there was to it—so simple but it worked, and the boys did a great job. They felt that they had earned the right to stay up late and they were proud of themselves. Using this request reversal wasn't done with deception or selfish intentions. It was simply a helpful strategy to assist in less-stressful compliance. Other conversations might look like this:

CJ "Can I go to the milk bar with Josh, Mum?"

Me "Sure, just grab those bins in first and that will be

fine."
CJ "Can you make us a hot Milo, Mum?"
Me "Sure, if you just feed Patch please, I'll get it ready."

Often, compliance just comes down to how we word things. Simply reversing the order of our words can be enough. Give something to work toward rather than starting a losing battle. Try these:

> **Instead of:** *"You'll lose your pocket money if you don't behave."*
> **Change to:** *"You'll earn your pocket money if you keep up this good behaviour."*

> **Instead of:** *"If you don't dry those dishes, you won't be able to watch TV."*
> **Change to:** *"If you get the dishes done quickly, you can watch TV with Dad and me."*

> **Instead of:** *"If you're naughty in the shops, we won't be getting Maccas for lunch."*
> **Change to:** *"Thanks for helping. Let's get the shopping done, then have Maccas for lunch."*

Almost the same words but with a very different message. The first sets convey a threat and preconceived expectation of misbehaviour. Straight away a child's attitude will change, and their self-esteem will plummet. Alternatively, the second sets hold the promise of good things to come for doing what is expected. A friendly attitude promotes anticipation of being rewarded and better behaviour. As adults, we all know how we'd rather be spoken to, so let's get into the helpful habit of rephrasing some of our words to convey a more positive message.

THE B WORD

I must admit, I did use bribery once on CJ, and yes it was a very definite bribe. There's no other way to put it, and I admit it freely with no excuses. CJ needed to have braces, but he was absolutely adamant that he would not, under any circumstances, have them. Other than putting him under general anaesthetic to even get him to an appointment in regard to braces, I didn't know how I would get his cooperation.

At the time, snake-boards (cool skateboard-type contraptions) were the must-have item for boys. CJ had begun saving for one, but they were priced at over a hundred dollars. To CJ, on $5 a week pocket money budget, this seemed like a galaxy away. So yes, I told him if he had the braces put on without any issue, I would pay for the rest of the snake-board. Of course, Mr Here-and-now-don't-think-of-the-consequence-CJ jumped at that offer.

The day came. The braces went on, and afterward we picked up the much-coveted snake-board. Probably silly on my part considering he could have fallen off it and knocked out his teeth, but he didn't. Though his snake board exuberance wore off

after a few months, his braces were there to stay …
for the next three years.

USING OBVIOUS CONSEQUENCES:

While all this requesting and rewarding sounds great,
of course, we can't always reward a child when
they're misbehaving or not complying. This is when
a firm, but fair message needs to be given, pointing
out the consequences of their behaviour. We can still
be on their side while explaining consequences. It
doesn't have to be a conflict situation.

Not wearing their bike helmet:

*"If you don't wear your helmet, I can't allow you ride
your bike, and I know how much you like to."*

*Or "I'd hate for you to get hurt. If you did, then you
wouldn't be able to ride anywhere!"*

*Or even, "You can get fined for not wearing one. That
would use up three months pocket money!" (He later
did and that natural consequence worked wonders!).*

Being nasty to visiting children:

*"If you can't play nicely, you won't be allowed to have
friends over next time you ask. It's only for another
hour, so try to get along, and I'll be very proud of you"
said with a hug.*

*Or "You don't have to play with Sally and Tom, but
please don't be nasty either, because then you'll have
to play in your room, and I know you want to stay out*

here with us," said calmly and in private.

Our ADHD children can be very intelligent, but the problem is that they act first and think later, or sometimes not at all. We need to give them clear choices that will prompt them to make a good and correct decision. In a more serious situation giving two clearly opposing alternatives can be very effective. These are choice's we give when there really is no choice.

About to punch his sister:

1st choice: Punch her, get into big trouble, get sent to bed early and possibly grounded—No fun at all.

2nd choice: Don't' punch her, and let her be the naughty one. Come and tell us what she said or did. We'll reprimand her if needed, and be proud of you.

Refusing to get dressed for school:

1st choice: Okay, don't get dressed, then you'll be late so there will be no TV this morning. We'll both be annoyed and have a bad start to the day.

2nd choice: Get dressed as quickly as you can. I'll help you to get started. You'll be able to watch your favourite show, and we'll have a good morning together.

Be creative and devise choices that your child will

best respond to. They should be straightforward alternatives that clearly explain both the best and the worst possible scenarios.

NATURAL CONSEQUENCES

We can also just allow natural consequences to occur such as not taking a coat and then getting cold. They'll remember consequences that they've experienced more than those we just tell them about. Cruel to be kind, as the saying goes.

One week, CJ was continuously nagging me to let him ride his skateboard to school. "You're not allowed. It's a school rule, no skateboards," I would tell him.

"Yes, I am!" he countered.

And it went and on and on. So, one day I just let him take it. What happened? He was told he wasn't allowed to have a skateboard at school, and the teacher confiscated it for the day. In this case, rather than me protecting him from getting into trouble, I let the natural consequences occur. Outcome: He never asked again.

It's easy to overprotect our children, but they will learn more from these valuable life-lessons than we could ever tell them. There will be times that we need to point out for them what the obvious consequences will be, but it's always better if it can be done in a non-threatening way with encouragement rather than intimidation.

Threats are convenient to use. They are easy to think up, they get our point across quickly, and they effectively convey our anger and frustration. I used them many times, but their effectiveness was only temporary and at a significant cost. It fostered resentment and a lack of respect. I discovered the more threats I issued, the more defiant CJ became, the opposite result of what I'd had in mind.

'Just do it' type demands rarely work with ADHD kids so using motivation can be our most valuable tool. We don't want our children to just grudgingly do what we ask. We want them to *want to do* what we ask of them, and to understand our reasoning—so eventually, they too will share our values, not because we said they have to, but through their own choice.

TRAVEL TIPS:

- Motivate by pointing out the good.
- Put your requests in reverse gear.
- Explain consequences to see the road ahead.

10. DISCIPLINE—PUNISHMENT VS CORRECTION

"Before passing judgement, consider—the worst of decisions are often made with the best of intentions."

Discipline is an area where it can be hard to find a balance between being too soft or being too harsh, being a pushover or being a tyrant. It can also be an area where we unwittingly make our worst mistakes. With CJ being my first child, I used my own upbringing as my measure when it came to discipline. I assumed that he would do as I asked, be polite, say sorry when he'd done wrong and be kind and considerate of other people as I had (from memory anyway!). During my own childhood, whatever mum and dad said was how it was, and my brother and I wouldn't dare to question that. Therefore, my own experience was really no guide for rearing my live-wire, ever-questioning son.

I loved being a mum and was quiet and easy-going, so I couldn't understand why CJ was basically my opposite. I worried that if I didn't discipline him enough as a child that he would still be regarded as one of those 'naughty kids' as he grew older. I mistakenly thought that being harder on him would improve his behaviour. I would see other parents using threats and strict punishments that seemed to keep their children in line, so I thought 'okay, this is what I'm supposed to do. If I'm hard on him, he'll toe the line, right?' ...but our line was never going to be *toed* that way. It was, stretched, walked over and often broken. Punishments gave the opposite result of what I was aiming for. They gave me a defiant and resentful child. This was mostly because CJ didn't think his behaviour was inappropriate. As far as he was concerned, he was just being himself and was he was generally clueless as to why I was angry with him.

While a non-ADHD child might think twice after a reprimand, and then do better to try and please their parents, CJ's attitude just became 'oh, well'. It just reinforced his belief that he was unfairly treated. Unintentionally, I was worsening CJ's behaviour with my well-meaning strictness.

"That's it! You aren't watching any TV tonight! I'm not taking you shopping again! Go and say sorry right now!" What I was in fact doing was just mirroring CJ's bad temperament, a temperament that I didn't like in him and one that he liked even less in me. How was that right for me when it was the exact behaviour I was trying to discourage? I couldn't see the irony at the time. He soon became self-protective and would put up his walls like an invisible force field to keep me out. Clearly, this firmness was not the road to take, so another route had to be found, and it was found by way of correction.

PARTY PERILS

By the time CJ was five, we were often invited to the birthday parties of friends and neighbours' children. While the other mums would be drinking coffee and chatting, I would usually spend the whole time following my CJ around for fear that he would hit, push or annoy the other little partygoers. Sister Shari was only three, so I'd be watching her as well.

At one such party, for just a few seconds I took my eagle-eyes off my son. Suddenly a child began screaming as if evil swamp monsters had suddenly appeared (but no such luck!).

"CJ pushed Tim off the slide and took Rachel's bucket!" a child yelled. A blonde pony-tailed girl appeared to be crying, waiting for said bucket's return. As other parents turned to look, embarrassed, I immediately launched into: "CJ, you naughty boy, go and say sorry. You don't do that!"

Of course, he had no intention of saying sorry, so I took him to one side and whispered angrily. "How could you do this? Can't you just behave? Can't we ever have one day out without you being naughty? That's it, we're going home!"

CJ was outraged and put on his best huffy five-year-old pout, protesting the unfairness of waiting for slides and buckets. We quickly said our goodbyes and made our escape. The kids were both upset. Shari had been having fun playing, and to CJ this was pretty much a normal occurrence, but I just wanted to leave, to go far away from all the 'normal people' and their better-behaved children. There were no positives that day. I went home angry and embarrassed. CJ went home angry and resentful. Shari was disappointed yet again. The whole day seemed ruined.

Some may say that I didn't do anything wrong in disciplining him, but I did. I forgot that there is a real little person with real feelings inside that 'naughty little boy' exterior. My problem was that there was always an incident and it always *appeared* to be CJ's fault. I was always on edge and this was colouring my thinking.

At first glance, it may seem that CJ was just naughty, but instead of jumping to the same old conclusions I should have dug a little deeper. I could have handled things better. Often, it's more our embarrassment, rather than the actual situation that flusters us, and then we react impulsively. This generally results in chaos or tears. So, what should I have done? I should have used correction and it was as simple as A-D-H-D:

A IS FOR 'ASK': ASK YOUR CHILD CALMLY WHAT HAPPENED.

CJ's answer might have gone something like this: "I wanted to go down the slide, but Tim was climbing up it and wouldn't get off, so I went down anyway, and he fell off when I went under his legs. Then

Rachel called me a big idiot, and she said she was going to hit me with her bucket, so I grabbed it".

D IS FOR 'DEFUSE': DEFUSE THE SITUATION.

I might say something like, "If that's what happened, then I understand why you took the bucket, but you've accidentally hurt Tim". I would then encourage CJ to ask if Tim was okay and to say sorry. If he won't apologise (and being the defiant CJ that he was, he probably wouldn't have), I would ask Tim myself, if he was alright. This would usually be enough to finish the situation, and the other mums would see that everything was under control (and the offending bucket was moved out of sight).

H IS FOR 'HELP': HELP YOUR CHILD THROUGH THE SITUATION

Rather than leaving the party, or over-reacting and embarrassing him, I could have taken CJ aside and helped him to find another activity or another child to play with while we waited for the slide to be free. Redirection is wonderful!

D IS FOR 'DISCUSS': DISCUSS ALTERNATIVES WITH YOUR CHILD.

With everything calm, we could talk about

alternatives such as doing something else until Tim was finished, or asking him *nicely* to move, or coming to mum for help in getting a turn. If he really felt the need to retaliate when Rachel called him a big idiot, he could say something back like, "What you say is what you are," then walk away and let Rachel be the 'naughty one'. Of course, he might not see the benefit in this, so I could explain that parties will be more fun if he's not the one in trouble and that I'd be proud of him.

A few minutes spent doing a mini post-mortem on an issue is time well spent. A child won't be so much on the defensive if they feel their side is being heard. They will learn better ways to cope, and one incident won't ruin a whole day.

POSITIVE PLANNING

Parties, school events or any social situation can be a trial for our ADHD children when they try to fit in with unfamiliar children in a restrictive environment. They may have to sit still, wait their turn for food, or take turns in a game. It's not easy for our children to adhere to birthday party etiquette for a long period of time. That said, always expect their best. Don't bring your child into a party with a long list of *don'ts*. (Don't yell, don't push, don't be greedy). It's as if we provoke bad behaviour by suggestion. "You'd better not run around," or "You better not act silly". This would put anyone in a bad mood, the opposite result to what we want.

Approach outings with a positive attitude and prepare for situations in advance. Before the event, roleplay situations that might occur, so they're fresh in your child's mind: "Now, how would you ask for another party pie?" or "How would we ask to join in a game?" Most of the time they don't mean to be annoying (occasionally they do!), but often they don't realise that their behaviour isn't acceptable.

Keep watch for potential problems. It might be a power play over a toy mower, an impending fight over who gets the last cupcake, or they're about to fall into the water feature while trying to catch an imaginary fish. We can *subtly* intervene by redirecting our child to the correct behaviour or just to another activity. Redirection is a great tool. If you see a situation arising, send them off to do a job for you. "CJ, can you please run and get me my purse for the lunch orders?"

If they're becoming restless get them to help you with something. "CJ, can you help me with reaching the top shelf. I'll lift you up."

If a conversation is heading in the wrong direction, completely change the subject. As the boys are threatening each other, look around for a distraction and use it. "Hey, look at those butterflies by the window! Go and see if you can find any more … Oh, they must have flown away!"

If they're climbing a much too tall tree, help them down with care, just as you would a toddler climbing on a table, and as if it's expected, rather than broken record style: "CJ, that's enough. CJ, what have I told you? CJ, come here!" Phrases such as these rarely worked. CJ would just laugh and climb higher, so I would use the surprise attack of care, correction and distraction. "Careful, honey. You could fall! Quick come with me for a piggyback." "Oh look, the party pies are ready!" All said with a smile, knowing that two minutes well spent on a piggyback would save us from a ten-minute yelling match, and possibly a broken arm!

Of course, correction may not always be enough. There needs to be consequences (aka punishments) for certain situations, and it helps if they know consequences in advance.

DISCIPLINED DISCIPLINE

We need to be disciplined with our discipline, not inconsistent. I must admit I started out as a wishy-washy disciplining parent. Being a softie, I didn't like to be the bad guy and would often half-heartedly and impulsively threaten in frustration, but never carry out these threats. By following through only sometimes, and not at other times, a child doesn't know where they stand. They will try to challenge you if there is a slight possibility that you'll weaken or become confused and angry when you do follow through.

CJ came to understand that I rarely meant what

I said and that my empty threats had little effect. "Right, keep that up, and we're not going to the zoo!" I'd say, for example, when the four of us were ready to go out the door. Even though CJ and Shari were fighting, they knew we'd still be going. Of course Mum wouldn't do that to them. It was just an empty threat. Empty threats just make us feel better; as if we do have control even when we have no intention of following through. If it's said, we should be prepared to carry it out.

CJ's dad, while a lot firmer than me, would also do the same and often not follow through on punishments. CJ would be yelling at his sister for an imagined injustice, and Bob would suddenly bellow, "Right, that's it! Get to bed". CJ would quieten down and continue to play, ignoring the 'get to bed' instruction, and usually, nothing would happen.

When Bob actually did send him to bed, CJ went down kicking and screaming, protesting that it was unfair because he didn't usually have to go to bed when dad said he had to and he should have been warned that his dad actually meant it!

ENSURE THEY KNOW EXACTLY WHAT THEY'RE BEING PUNISHED FOR.

We can send them to their room so often that it becomes the norm, and they just retreat there on auto-pilot (Pleased to be away from the cranky grown-ups anyway). We might have spent five minutes lecturing them, and they've just zoned out (just like we might ignore with a whining child). When we go back to check if they've thought about things, they reply, "Um, what things?" with a bewildered look as if we've just asked them to explain the meaning of life. You may have to remind them why they were punished in the first place.

MAKE CONSEQUENCES IMMEDIATE WHERE POSSIBLE AND SUITABLE FOR THE OFFENCE.

If they won't get ready for school and just stare at the TV, turn the TV off. Simple and direct. If they're rude to you when they come out from school, don't let them sit in the front of the car. If they're acting silly in a shop and correction hasn't worked, don't allow that treat you were going to buy them. If homework isn't done, no games or TV until it is. If fighting or being disruptive, sit quietly for five minutes near mum or dad.

Do stick to the point. Don't bring up past mistakes. Don't use sarcasm unless you want to teach them this. Do act like an adult, not just a bigger naughty child. If a consequence or punishment is required, be firm but fair. Don't use extremes you can't enforce like 'you're grounded for a month'. That's really never going to happen, is it? I once made the mistake of using a ten-hour-later-type punishment. "Right, that's it! Six o'clock bedtime tonight!" I exclaimed, maniacally scribbling the punishment on an old envelope and attaching it to a parrot fridge magnet—my own mini version of, "So, there! Take that!" (Just like a naughty child).

CJ then left to go to school on his bike. Unbeknown to me he had taken my 'angry punishment note' off the fridge. A few minutes later he came back, knocking on the front door to confess his sin. Much as he shouldn't have taken it, I couldn't help softening when I realised his little conscience had told him to come back and 'fess up'. That was a good thing, I had clearly overreacted (I think I broke the pen) and CJ had just proved to me he was indeed a good kid, so I weighed it up. CJ's 'Morning Silliness Rating' had been maybe a 7 out of 10, but his 'do the Right Thing Rating' had just come in at a heart-warming 10 out of 10. I let him off. The good outweighed the bad and to be honest, my earlier 'Parental Overreaction Rating' would have come in at a whopping 10 out of 10 with my 'Sensible Parent Punishment Rating' at a disappointing 1 out of 10. Sometimes they do deserve that second chance, but it can also double as a second chance for mad morning mums.

We often react in a certain way because it is what we think we're supposed to do. We see other parents doing the same thing and follow suit, however with our ADHD kiddies, we need to be open to trying different approaches. Children can even help in making up the consequences so that they feel involved and everyone knows what to expect when rules aren't followed. Often, our kids can think up better ones that we can, like "No dessert tonight!" (Hmm ... Do we even usually have dessert?)

Alternatively, take them aside for a few minutes of quiet time. Try a correction talk, but otherwise make any consequence as immediate as possible so it can pass and a chance to start over can be presented, the slate clean. Our children should be secure in the knowledge that they can always come to us and be heard; that if they feel angry, frustrated or overwhelmed that we will always listen; that we will try to help even if we don't agree with them.

It isn't necessary to have a punishment for every wrong-doing. Punish too often, and the effectiveness will eventually decrease, but by practising the more effective *correction,* those wrong-doings will eventually decrease.

Our children can very definitely push our buttons (even buttons we didn't know we had), but we have been granted the all-important task of setting the better example; of teaching them the consequences of their words and actions: not to be judge and jury, but to be guardians and guides, to correct, to love and protect.

TRAVEL TIPS:

- Ask for the story before acting in frustration.
- Harsh punishment = resentment and repeats.
- Caring correction = support and alternatives.

11. SOCIAL SKILLS—THE BASICS

"Practise, practise—then practise some more."

Social skills don't often come easily for our ADHD children. The things we take for granted, the things most kids pick up on early, don't always come so effortlessly to ours. They can be bossy and over-friendly, moody and withdrawn or loud and overexcited, causing other children to shy away from them. School and social situations can be overwhelming for any child, but even more so for a child with the unpredictable traits of ADHD.

Think of our kids as having their Learner's plates on. One or two lessons won't be enough to pass the test. It's going to take an ongoing series of lessons. Some will pick it up fast; others may need more lessons and more time to become competent in their social skills.

We often just expect that our children will pick up the ways of the world. We think that we shouldn't have to teach them many basic things. They should *just know* from observation of the world around them. Like waiting patiently, like not touching things that don't belong to them, like not interrupting conversations. But if your child is continually making the same mistakes, losing self-esteem and friends, always the one in trouble, there are many strategies to help them to relate better to others. We can teach by role-playing and by example, and we have a wealth of experience to share.

SPEAKING OF SHARING

I was forever verbally jumping on CJ when I thought he was acting selfishly: "Did you take the last biscuit? Don't be so greedy! Can't you just share with your sister?"

I thought it was the best way to 'change him'. It wasn't. This negative reinforcement just brought down his spirits and made him even more defiant and self-protective. I realised I had to stop trying to be his conscience and to help him find his own, rather than trying to force one onto him.

One afternoon, I put out some leftover chocolate cake that I'd saved for the after-school snack. CJ saw it first and proceeded to take a large piece, leaving hardly any for the rest of us. My former naïve self would have berated him, but this time I pretended not to notice.

I called his younger siblings to give them their piece, feigning surprise at the small amount of cake left saying loudly, "Oh, I thought there was more cake than that, I was going to have a piece too. I'll have to wait until next time".

CJ looks at his cake and then at me. I'm not looking at him, but tidying up the empty plate. He walks over to me, quickly taking another bite so as not to show me how big his piece was, then he says, "Here, Mum, you can have a bite of mine (yes, just a bite)". I look appropriately appreciative.

"Oh, thanks, CJ. Are you sure?"

"Yeah, Mum. I want you to have some," he urges. I take what he has offered and thank him.

"That's okay," he says, proud of himself for 'sharing'.

Now, maybe that's not ideal, but it's a lot better than my early attempts at forcing him to feel guilty. What if I had said, "You always have to be greedy don't you? It's just too hard to share. Well, next time, you won't get any ..." While this is what I felt like saying, it wasn't going to do anything to change his behaviour. He would only resent me and become more self-protective. Letting him figure out for himself that he'd been a little greedy, and allowing him to try and rectify it was a step toward finding his own moral compass.

We can also encourage our non-share-loving children to share by sharing our own things with them and inspiring them to do likewise. A few extra minutes spent now can teach them lessons that last a lifetime. For example, you get a new laptop, and he wants to play with it on his own. Instead of a blanket 'no', alternatively, you could offer, "Would you like to help me with it?"

Or, for example, he gets a remote-controlled car. Even though you may have no interest, say, "Wow, great car mate. I'd love to have a turn." In this way, we can encourage our children to consider and choose to share, even when they're a little reluctant.

PATIENCE

Teaching patience can be a battle: waiting to speak in class, waiting for a turn on the slide, waiting for their turn at basketball, waiting in a line. You see a line of children at the schoolroom door, and there's always that one child falling out of line, stumbling, getting told off. Yes, that was usually CJ! Because our ADHD kiddies become bored so easily, we can help them to think up ideas to pass the time and learn to wait quietly. Again, rather than scolding, offer some ideas to 'stay out of trouble'. Talk to them about it. Acknowledge that you know it can be difficult for them: "I know it gets hard to stand in line, but it's usually only for a few minutes. What do you think you could do to pass the time?"

Help them to begin with, and then you might be surprised at what our creative kids can come up with themselves.

- See how many things you can see starting with the letter of your name.
- Watch for different birds that fly past if you're waiting outside.
- You could count and see how high a number you can get to.
- Count to yourself and work out how many minutes have passed until you go in.

Teach them the 'one Mississippi, two Mississippi' way or maybe they can choose their own word. 'One alligator, two alligators'.

As they're naturally distractible, we can use distraction in a positive way. When waiting in a long line, be it at the cinema, or for a ride at the fair, or waiting at the doctor's office: plan ahead and have something for them to do. It might be a small toy to fiddle with or a riddle book to read together. We often played *Noughts and Crosses* while waiting for appointments. These 'waiting' times are great opportunities for bonding.

As children get older, take a puzzle book and enjoy it together. CJ loved the challenge of the IQ puzzle books. Another old favourite was 'I spy'. Anytime we had to wait, be it at the doctor's, in the grocery line or just on a long drive 'I Spy' was the go-to-game to stop backseat squabbles. My kids thought it was simply for fun, but it was really to make waiting easier, seemingly quicker and much less stressful.

Our ADHD children tend to blurt things out and can find it hard to contain themselves when they have an idea or something to say. Practise waiting to speak at home with an egg timer and see how long they can go without talking. Make it a competition with other family members and have a prize for the longest 'shoosher'. Maybe even a family record to beat. Our kids will learn that they can have control when they choose to, and this will flow into the classroom and social settings.

Play games where you need to take turns. Old-style board games are great for this, like *Ludo*, *Connect Four*, *Snakes and Ladders*, or *Monopoly* and *Family Feud'* when they're older. It's easy to give children their own game console or tablet, but with these, everything is immediate; they don't learn the important skill of waiting and letting someone else have their turn.

MANNERS

Using manners seems easy enough right? Our kids see us using manners all the time, but we can't just assume they know the drill. Learning manners can seem like learning another language to our kids. They think they're getting it, and then suddenly things are different. It can be confusing for our children when we suddenly 'forget' our own manners. We might tell our child to "Quick, get in the car" (we don't have to say please, do we?). Or we impatiently tell our child to "Move!" when they're in our way (umm, where did excuse me go?).

Be aware of your own manners. There no point trying to teach a child correct behaviours if we adults don't adhere to the same standard. Point out and praise your child when they use manners correctly, to reiterate their importance and your appreciation.

Until they're off their 'manners learner plates, it's helpful to place reminders of the basics in a prominent place where your child can see them each day. Make up a list —yes, another! (or buy a pre-made chart). It might look something like this:

- **Please:** When asking for —anything at any time, for someone to move out of the way, to join a game, or for something to eat. Also known as the magic word.

- **Thank you:** When anyone does something for you, or gives something to you when given a compliment, when you leave a friend's house, or when Patch gives you his paw.

- **You're welcome:** When someone thanks you. ☺

- **I'm sorry:** When you bump into someone, hurt someone's feelings or damage someone's property. To show others that you care.

- **Excuse me:** To get someone's attention, to speak to them, to get past someone. Also for sneezing, burping, accidental laughs or any other weird noise emitted!

- **Pardon:** For when you don't hear someone properly, sounds better than "what?" Can replace 'Excuse me' for weird noises as above.

- **Washing hands:** Before meals, after playing with pets, after going to the toilet, if they look dirty, if you pick your nose ... eww!

- **At the dinner table:** Use cutlery not fingers, don't talk with your mouth full, ask to leave the table, don't poke sister in the eye with fork pretending to be a pirate (CJ!).

Practising manners doesn't have to be boring. It *can* be fun. Have your child come up with their own suggestions. Even a list of what not to do! For better table manners you can have your child help to cook a family dinner, and you can be the 'guest'. 'Forget' some of your own manners and have your child tell *you* when you slip up.

Eating out is great practice for using manners; make it a short stay if you must. Give them the responsibility of ordering to also encourage this social skill. It's a good idea to limit food choices. If there are too many options, our ADHD kiddies can find it difficult to choose and constantly change their mind. Give clear but limited choices, so they feel it's their decision. For example, you're at a café for lunch. Instead of "What do you want to eat?" change it to "Would you like a salad roll, a pizza or a hamburger?" Three good choices and not twenty minutes spent looking at the menu with them changing their mind half a dozen times.

INTRODUCTIONS

Meeting and greeting can be confusing for our kiddies. One day we might expect our child to be 'seen and not heard' when we bump into a friend as we rush about our day. The next time we expect them to say hello, but they either remain quiet or act silly for attention. Always introduce them as you would any other person. It only takes a moment and lets them know that they're important too. They'll then be less likely to misbehave. Rehearse this at home. Use different examples of what to say and do. Be clear on what you expect, and keep it simple. Three simple expressions will get them by initially when they're younger. 'Hello,' 'Nice to meet you' and 'Goodbye'. They can build from there. Encourage them to look people in the eye, that little touch makes all the difference. Let them know you'll be happy with that, and then they're off the hook!

LISTENING

Actively encourage your child's listening skills. You can practise with them by repeating what each other has said until it becomes a habit to absorb the other person's words. This may seem obvious, but often *the obvious* is what they miss. They hear other adults and us talking so much around them that voices become background noise.

Remind them that they need to listen to other speakers and think about what they're saying, just as they would want others to listen to them. Remind them that they might miss important information such as instructions for homework, what time karate practice is, or when being offered that last piece of chocolate cake

BEING LISTENED TO

CJ was generally very vocal (Okay yes, I mean excitably loud!). When he wanted to be heard, he would often yell rather than sensibly relaying what he needed to say. This would immediately put other people offside, as the yelling was heard before any intelligible words. I was constantly reminding him not to be so loud and to speak more slowly.

This was easy to forget so we came up with a little motto that was easy to use and remember. It was "Tell, don't yell". I explained that if he wanted people to be annoyed and not listen, he could yell, but if he wanted people to listen to him, he should speak more calmly. "You listen better when Mum *tells,* but you don't really listen when Mum *yells*, right?" So, when CJ became overly vocal, I'd use this little phrase, his memory would be jogged, and this would prompt him to tone himself down if he wanted to be heard.

Our kids tend to get the blame, even when things aren't their fault. Other children know who's usually in trouble and that the adults will most likely believe that 'CJ did it!' CJ would then fall head-first into the trap of yelling, "No, I didn't! You're a liar!" thereby inadvertently becoming the troublemaker that he wasn't (necessarily) in the first place.

We can help them to avoid this by encouraging them to speak rationally rather than losing control, yelling and looking guilty. Using easily remembered mottos as cues, such as our 'Tell don't yell' motto is a great habit to adopt. Simple, to the point, and it gives a child the opportunity to stop, think and try again (though be prepared for them to use it on you too!).

Apologies

CJ could get himself into trouble in the blink of an eye. Often, unintentionally, things would go awry. He could be laughing, running and looking backwards then accidentally knock over another child. He could be playing pirates in the lounge room, and a glass coffee table gets smashed (we lost three before I used my brain and bought a wooden one!).

"Say sorry!" we demand, and then we get a half-hearted parrot-like apology in return. There's no point forcing a child to say sorry when he thinks he's done no wrong. Have the conversation. Point out exactly what they did, why it was wrong and help them to acknowledge their mistake or actions. If it's an accident, they happen to everyone, and a genuine sorry is all that needed. If it was something deliberate and they apologise sincerely, the conflict can be over, and they'll feel better. When you point out that apologising is good for them and can end a bad situation, they'll be more likely to say sorry rather forcing it.

CJ might be jumping around, trip over a school bag and bump into another child. Both boys get annoyed and start pushing each other. CJ is blamed for causing a fight thus confirming his attitude of 'the world is so unfair'. If CJ's immediate reaction was to say sorry, it might have been a different story. It's also important that our children see us apologising when we have done wrong. If I had been in a bad mood and were extra grumpy with the kids, I'd think about it and then go and apologise. Yes, I'd apologise to a nine-year-old, a seven-year-old or a four-year-old! "Sorry, honey. Mummy didn't mean to be grumpy with you, and it wasn't fair." They will feel valued and respected and by your example, will learn that apologies are a good thing.

JOINING IN PLAY

Our kids can go either way when it comes to social interactions. They can be pushy and just 'power through' a group of children playing, or they might stand back thinking no one wants them to play. If they're having trouble, explain how to start off slowly by being interested and friendly. They might first ask about what children are playing, and then ask to play or join in without taking over the game or the conversation. Point out that they have many interesting and likeable qualities and will make for a good friend just by being themselves.

If they tend to be bossy or even a bully, help them to see and feel the result of their actions and words by using roleplay. Pretend to be the bully: "Hey, give me that ball. I'm playing now!" Ask if they like this bully version of you. Hopefully, they won't like bully *you* and realise that people won't like the bully version of them either. The door is then open for discussion on why being bossy isn't good for them, and to talk about and encourage better choices.

GIVING GENUINE COMPLIMENTS

Our kids can be quite self-absorbed, so it helps to encourage them to see good qualities in other people. For younger children, it's a good way to teach appreciation, and for older children, it will help when building friendships and relationships. Ask them to think of something nice about another family member that is deserving of a compliment. Take in turns complimenting each other, and rather than being envious of what another has, say something nice about it. This is also an opportunity to practise saying thank you and accepting the compliment. They may not see the point at first, but they will soon figure it out when they see the smiles and good feelings generated. They can carry that skill into the schoolyard and other social settings.

Instead of trying to grab Johnny's new football and run off with it, they might say, "I like your football Johnny, is it new?" (Then hopefully not run off with it anyway!). All being well, they'll get a positive response and maybe a kick of the prized football to-boot. Instead of being envious that Ruby was chosen as the class captain, they could instead congratulate her and receive a 'thank you' in return. Seeing what a difference their words and actions can make is a great experience for our children.

The simple ability to read facial expressions (the clues to what others are thinking and feeling) is sometimes lost on our ADHD children. They're often so full of energy that they fail to notice smaller details such as when other children or teachers are becoming frustrated and annoyed.

They can go on and on in their own little world without realising others are becoming hurt or upset, impatient or even angry with them. Before they know it, a teacher has reprimanded them, another parent has yelled at them, or another child has hit out at them, and their response is: "Huh? What did I do?" Our oblivious ADHD child had no idea it was coming. Fortunately, this is an easy skill to practise at home in a fun way to show our kids what others may be thinking or feeling. Make it a game; pull some faces, put on some expressions. Write up some cue cards to pick from. Start out easy: 'happy,' 'sad,' 'angry,' 'upset'. Then move onto harder ones like 'sulking,' 'disbelieving', and all the way up to 'about-to-snap'. They can then make their own expressions and test you. Recognising these facial cues will help them to be more aware of those around them and learn to adjust their behaviour accordingly, making life a little easier.

Some social skills will come naturally. Others won't, and it's often the simple ones we least expect. They'll need to be unlocked like a safe that needs opening. Our children can't know what they don't know, until they have that combination to see and learn for themselves. Theory alone isn't always enough, like when we need to change a tyre, for example, and it's done for us with just a brief explanation. Then the next time it happens, we need help again because we still don't know exactly what to do to get the result we want for ourselves. Role play is effective because it gives children a chance to work things out for themselves in the safe haven of home with the guidance of the people they love and trust most. It's a fun way to put theory into practice for essential skills they will carry with them into the big wide world.

TRAVEL TIPS:

- Be aware of your own manners.
- Don't assume a child 'just knows'.
- Test drive their social skills at home.

12. SOCIAL SKILLS—SELF-AWARENESS AND FORESIGHT

"Behaviours can't be changed until they're identified and understood."

Self-awareness and foresight are intertwined with our ability to handle social situations, and the same goes for our children, especially when it comes to dealing with negative feelings, conflict, anger and aggression. CJ generally thought he was always right, that the world was generally unfair, and that everybody else was wrong. This made for an often-angry child. I came to realise that it was important for him to be aware when he began to feel angry or annoyed. Just as I could, he could learn to recognise that sudden bad thought, the growing irritation, the clenched fist or gritted teeth. That's if he got that far. Sometimes those feelings were all rolled up into a few seconds before he would act out, either verbally or physically.

It's normal for our children to feel like this. We all do at times. It's what they choose to do about the feeling that matters the most. Their actions bring consequences and outcomes that can be good or bad. Self-awareness and foresight are skills that we can teach to help them alter outcomes for the better. We can talk about the different feelings that can cause conflict situations such as jealousy, resentment and anger, in order to cope with common triggers. "Why does Shari get to sit in the front?" "The other kids won't let me play!" "Why can't I go with Dad?"

We can explain that these are all normal feelings and their siblings and friends can feel this way too. Ask them what consequences might come from acting irrationally based on their negative feelings. Maybe their actions will lead to being in trouble with mum and dad, being grounded or having to leave a party early. Possibly it will mean they will get frequent school detentions and gain a bad reputation. No positives here. Then talk about the alternatives. Explain the benefits of better behaviour and responses. For example, Mum and Dad will be pleased with them. They won't have to leave the party early. They won't be grounded. They won't feel embarrassed.

Of course, this is age-dependent, and while it may not stop every angry outburst, they will have some awareness as to how to arrive at a better decision. We have a great platform at home to teach this type of self-awareness and foresight within our children's sibling relationships and the issues that commonly arise.

One afternoon eleven-year-old CJ and four-year-old brother Harry had constantly been fighting. I could hear them outside yelling at each other. I warned them both what would happen if they didn't stop. I appealed to CJ's pride saying that now he was eleven and too big to fight like a preschooler. I thought it had worked, but soon I heard more yelling, so I went to split them up. Before I reached them, I could see CJ raising his arm as if to throw something, undoubtedly as hard as he could at his little brother. Ahh, too late! CJ's aim was, unfortunately, spot-on.

I ran to comfort Harry who was now crying, while CJ was just looking annoyed that he'd been caught. I then did all the things that I advise against! I grabbed CJ by the arm in a death grip, told him what a naughty boy he was. I yelled at him to go to his room and not to come out. He yelled back at me twice as loud of course. It was his brother's fault; he hated him and me. He stomped angrily to his room. Belatedly I asked Harry what had happened. He said with four-year-old honesty that he threw a wooden hand broom at CJ, but it missed and then CJ threw it back, only harder.

I was still fuming. CJ was the older one, he should behave better, but then it occurred to me I am even older, and I should behave even better again. I went to CJ's room, asked him to think about what had happened, and then I'd be back to talk to him. I went back after a few minutes with a blank sheet of paper and a pen and asked him to write down a few very important things.

I asked CJ to write:
- What he did and why he did it.
- Why he shouldn't have done it.
- Three things he could have done instead.

Either way that this went, it was good to work on his handwriting skills. Meanwhile, I talked to four-year-old Harry about throwing things. Not long after CJ called me in to show me his answers.

This is what he wrote:

- I threw a mini broom at Harry because he threw it at me.
- I shouldn't have done it because I hurt him, and I got into trouble.
- I could have told Harry first not to throw it, told Mum what he did, or stopped playing with him.

Getting CJ to write these solutions down helped him to think more clearly and to be more aware of what he'd done. It helped him to reflect on his actions and to realise that he did have choices. I told him that I was pleased with what he had written and next time to stick to what he knows in his heart and head that he should do. Any of his three alternatives would have been better. Some good had come from this bad incident. In this way, we can show children that they do have some control over a situation.

PLAYGROUND TOOLS

The playground can be a difficult place to navigate for our ADHD children. They need to run around and burn off energy, but still fit in and engage with other children. If it's organised games that involve taking a turn, this can be difficult and test their patience. A hundred years ago, maybe, they would have had fisty-cuffs, and it would have been quite acceptable, but not today. Give them the 'tools' to avoid an incident with another child. Talk about ways to diffuse their anger such as just saying to themselves 'that's enough' and walking away, going to get a drink of water, or finding a teacher before they lose their temper. Let them know it's okay to take their own timeout, even go for a run around the yard.

Give them some simple questions that they can ask themselves when they're tempted to lose control or do the wrong thing. For a younger child, their question may be, "Is this what Mum or Dad would want me to do?"

If 'yes', okay great, if 'no', don't do it. If you're not sure, just ask. Older children can ask themselves, "What's the right thing to do?" Even we adults often can't decide what to do at times, but this question will always give us the right answer even if it's not what we personally want. Explain that this is always for the best even if it doesn't seem so at the time. Let them know that you trust them to make a good decision (even if not yet totally convinced). If they're not sure of the right thing to do, tell them to make their best decision, and they won't be punished for good intentions.

ENCOURAGE CONSCIENCE

Encouraging their own sense of right and wrong will help ADHD children to behave better and monitor themselves in social environments, be it with family, friends, at school or just at home. Often, CJ wouldn't have done something that he was supposed to do (surprise, surprise) and even though I knew it, I wouldn't let on, opting for a more effective strategy.

One Saturday (pocket money day) CJ said he had finished his room. I knew he had put his clothes and rubbish under the bed, but I told him, "Great job, CJ. I knew you could do it," and I gave him a big hug and a kiss. I then said that now I was able to get all his washing done since he had put all his clothes into the laundry and I would vacuum his floor for him now that the rubbish was in the bin. I said how proud of him I was, and I would come and have a look at his lovely room in a few minutes. I gave him another hug, and a 'thank you'. I could see him squirming inside, and he said would I just wait a minute while he double checked that he'd done everything.

With that, he raced down to his room. I heard doors opening and closing quickly and some clanging and banging noises. He had obviously retrieved the dirty clothes from their hiding place and thrown them into the laundry, and he ran to the bin with a handful of old papers and rubbish when he thought I wasn't looking.

You could say I guilted him into this, but I prefer

to think that he chose to do the right thing, albeit with a little influence from mum. A step forward. If I'd immediately told him that he hadn't done a good enough job, or that I knew he was lying, it wouldn't have helped. It would have undoubtedly brought a defensive reaction from CJ about how unfair and mean I was and would have created yet another bad day. Allowing him time to rethink things for himself gave an often-needed second chance. We don't always have to 'know' everything. Their conscience might seem AWOL at times, but it's there. This was proven to me when my normally take-whatever-he can-get son was at the local shop buying his prized football cards.

TRUST IN YOUR TEACHING

I had sent CJ into a shop on his own for a bit of trust (or maybe because I was in sweatpants) and I waited in the car. He was taking a lot longer than I'd expected and I started to worry, imagining all sorts of silly things. Maybe he got side-tracked and was lost in the chocolate aisle. Maybe he was asking Neil, the shop-keeper, a thousand-and-one quick questions about football cards. Maybe he'd knocked over a display of tomato sauce and was sloshing around in it as he tried to explain. Even more ridiculous scenarios popped into my head, but then out he came with a big smile on his little face. "Mum, guess what! I got too much change back!" he yelled happily. I was about to launch into a complicated lecture on honesty when barely able to contain himself, he excitedly continued on, "And I told Neil, and he said thanks. Then he gave me extra football cards for being so honest!" CJ was beaming. I smiled, doing my best to hold back my happy tears.

"That's great CJ. I'm really proud of you."

There was nothing else to say. What a significant practical lesson he learnt that day, a lesson that honesty feels good and satisfying. And though he didn't expect it, his honesty did pay. And what a lesson I learnt, that I should give my son more credit. My 'not just naughty' child was able to do the right thing, all on his own.

USING CAMARADERIE

CJ's mind worked much the same as everybody else's, but he couldn't help blurting out any thought that was in his head, often as loudly as possible. He would end up in trouble yet again. Most mornings, I would hear the alarm and groan… "Ah, no. Time to get up. I want to stay in bed," I'd think to myself, but get straight up and get on with the day.

I'd wake up Shari, who was also probably thinking, "Oh, no, I don't want to get up. Not yet … I wish it was Sunday". But she looks up sleepily and just says. "Okay, Mum."

Next, I'd go to CJ's room. He looks at me and thinks the same as we did, but what does he do? He pulls the blankets over his head, refuses to get up and groans loudly. "Nooo! I don't want to! Go away! You always do this to me!" I'm immediately annoyed; CJ is in trouble again and so starts yet another bad morning. It occurred to me one day to tell him that we all feel this way. "Oh, really?" he said, surprised when I told him this. "I thought I was the only one who hated getting up."

I told him that we all do. We think exactly the same thing, but deal with it in a different way. Since he absolutely has to get out of bed, he should try to do as we do, to think those things but just not say it, at least don't yell it. Then I'll think he's 'being good'. He can still think his bad morning thoughts but not allow me to hear them, at least not as loudly. This was where he would get himself into trouble, not with his thoughts but with his actions. Making him aware of this helped him to tone himself down, at least a little bit.

CAUSE AND EFFECT

CJ, like most children, thought that most things were out of his control, that situations and conflicts 'just happened' and that what followed was just how it was. I wanted him to be aware that what he said or did, mattered very much and that he had the power to alter or choose an outcome.

A useful strategy was to encourage CJ to do the opposite of what he really felt like doing when angry or frustrated and to see what happened. It did take some coaxing, but it helped him to be aware of the power of his own words and actions, that he could have a strong influence over situations and that he could diffuse conflict.

When CJ had been in trouble with his dad, naturally his impulse afterward was to keep as far away as possible from his dad, to sulk or hide away in his room. One day, after they'd shared some hot-tempered words, I encouraged CJ to go and give his dad a hug and to say, 'I love you'. Even though this was the last thing CJ wanted to do (he would rather have thrown darts at his own head), I asked him to please try it for me and see what reaction he would get. It took a bit of coaxing, but since I was now the favourite parent (for a few minutes anyway), he finally agreed. He went up to his dad who, with an eerie similarity was also sulking, wrapped his little arms around his dad's waist and said tentatively, "Love you, Dad." As expected Dad softened, just a little, and replied gruffly (and maybe a little forced), "Love you too".

CJ grinned as he ran back to me. "It worked!" He exclaimed, "I think I'm out of trouble."

"See, you did that," I said. "You changed your Dad's mood!"

Just in that small gesture, he realised that things didn't just have to be a certain way and that with a little effort on his part, he could contribute toward changing a situation in a positive way.

EMPATHY AND CARING

We had a chart (on the fridge, of course) called the 'Caring Sharing Chart'. CJ and Shari were to let me know when they did something that made someone else happy or when someone did something to make them happy. We would then write it in on the chart. We aimed for at least one nice thing each day, and it was read over at the end of the week. It became great positive reinforcement that being a nice person is a good thing, not to mention a big boost for self-esteem. There was no chart for naughty things. We wouldn't want to be constantly reminded of foolish things we've done (and we've all done something at some point), and neither do our children. They were just dealt with at the time. By documenting the nice things they did, or the nice things that happened to them, weekly positive memories surpassed any bad ones.

We expect that empathy will just come naturally, but this quality can also be encouraged. CJ loved to be asked to figure things out, pleased to be included and responsible. If Shari or Harry were sick or sad, I would ask CJ, "What's something we could do to make them feel better?" By using 'we', he then wasn't solely responsible, but could work together with me to show care and compassion. If a friend has lost a pet, we can talk about how that friend must be feeling sad and discuss what we could do for them. "What's something nice we could do for Auntie Jean?"

Maybe, make a card or draw a picture. Inspire them to practise small kindnesses.

Let them experience how it feels to be compassionate by taking flowers to an elderly neighbour or even just helping a sibling to find a lost toy. Praise them, thank them, and they will feel proud of this appreciation and remember it. It can seem like a lot for our kids to take in with all this roleplay, encouragement and forward thinking, but with repetition, this will become habit and habit becomes a way of life, done without thinking.

We can only modify our behaviours when we're aware of them. It's harder for our children with little or no objectivity. They don't have decades of life experience to guide them, so this job falls to us. If your child just remembers a fraction of what you teach them about self-awareness, they'll be well on the way to achieving better relationships.

I used to think that with my never-ending words of advice and practical demonstrations, that CJ should be the smartest, most intuitive self-aware child in the universe; but it didn't seem that way, quite the opposite. It was as if I was explaining how to play *chess* to a chicken. I was doing a lot of talking, explaining, example-giving and tactic teaching for little success, and often wondered was it all in vain? It was only in the years ahead, that I realised CJ had taken in more than I had imagined. I came to hear my own words from his mouth. As an adult, he was talking about dealing with difficult people and said that he did so much negotiating that he could have been a hostage negotiator. The funny thing was, I used to say exactly the same thing about my interactions with him as a child. He added that people will treat you the way you treat them, and I wished I could have gone back and reassured 'young-mummy' me that my efforts were indeed, worthwhile.

TRAVEL TIPS:

- Change self-awareness from low-beam to high.
- Foresight will always beat hindsight.
- Practise kindness to encourage goodness.

13. TESTING TIMES

"Plan ahead—be prepared to change the plan."

Problem situations and testing times will come in all shapes and sizes, some expected and some unexpected; some minor and some that seem insurmountable, but there are many strategies and approaches to try. One size does not fit all, but with patience and planning, you will find your fit. On days when things are just going badly, with irritable, cranky kids or worse, an irritable, cranky mum, and with no positives in sight, it can feel like being on a fast-moving train heading in the wrong direction. The best thing to do is to get off that crazy train to nowhere. It's never too late to switch tracks and find a better direction for the day, to change trains and change the atmosphere and the mood to something more positive.

Imagine it's the school holidays. Your ADHD child is bouncing around like a kangaroo on a pogo stick, the other kids are bored and restless, and you're getting absolutely nothing done. Now, stop and say to yourself, "If we continue like this, the day will go from bad to worse. I'm getting angrier and more stressed with every minute. So, can the housework wait?" Well, the answer to that one is yes. It will be there today, tomorrow and the next day, but tomorrow or the next day you might not be as stressed and will be more productive. So, take charge and *change trains*.

Change the environment and see what happens. Tell the kids to get their shoes on, get out of the house and get out into the fresh air. If it's around lunch time, opt for fish-'n-chips at the beach or the park—this will be a stress release for you; no messy kitchen, and the kids will love it. Grab the dog and go for a walk or have a quick game of hide-and-seek in the backyard.

If the weather is bad, give everyone a half hour break; maybe a quick game of charades or start a jigsaw puzzle together. A quick happiness recharge then back to what you were doing in the world of must-dos, maybe with a promise to spring another mini fun break on them when they least expect it. It doesn't have to be for long, but it can turn a bad day around. Children love some impromptu fun and so will you. Even better it suits our impulsive, live-in-the-moment ADHD kiddies to a tee. They don't need to know your motives; just let them enjoy the treat, and you can enjoy the spoils.

POWER PLAY

Another problem situation is the dreaded 'power play', that dark parenting abyss that drags you in when you least expect it, but once you realise where you're heading, you can grab a foothold, climb to a safe place and control the escalation.

It was 8 am and almost time for ten-year-old CJ to leave for school on his bike. He was to be given a key to the house and to stay on his own for about fifteen minutes after school until I arrived home from work—this was good practice in trust and responsibility. Asked for the fourth time to put socks on, he lounges back on the couch and starts singing loudly in a fake voice to a song on the TV. I get annoyed, turn off the TV and take the socks from where he has now put them; on his hands (I guess I didn't specify exactly where he was to put them!). Immediately, he starts, "Don't you grab me, you hurt me," even though I hadn't.

Tactfully, I try to change the subject. "CJ, go and pack your lunch box into your schoolbag".

"Not unless you put the TV back on," he retorts defiantly. And there's the red flag; the road rage begins … and off I go!

"No, I will not! Just do as you're told, or I won't give you a key, and you can just sit on the doorstep until I get home," I threaten him. As expected, he retaliates immediately.

"I just won't go to school. I'll just ride around all day on my bike." He threatens back.

"Well, I'll be phoning your Dad if you don't do as you're told." Another threat.

Next comes the expected retaliation from CJ. "Then I'll run away and live somewhere else. You hate me anyway!"

Now, things are definitely out of control. We're both making threats and saying things we don't mean. Belatedly, I realise that I am doing exactly what I always tell myself not to do. I am letting him drag me into that dark place, a place I don't want to be. So, I stop and think about my next reaction. I then do what I should have done in the first place. I change my attitude. I sigh loudly with a smile, put my arm around CJ and say, "Honey, I want to trust you, and I know you can be responsible. All I ask is that you do what you are supposed to be doing like putting your socks on. I want to give you a key, but I need to know that I can trust you".

Confused by my sudden change in demeanour, I immediately have his attention and obviously relieved that the clash is over, he replies tentatively, "You can trust me. I promise"

I give him a kiss he gives me a hug and puts on his socks. That's all it took—me, the grown-up, to act like the grown-up. Duh!

You might be saying that I gave in to a ten-year-old with a very bad attitude, but I see it as not *giving in,* but taking charge of a volatile situation by stopping, thinking rationally and getting my son to listen to me. By speaking calmly like an adult (I sometimes forgot that I was one!), CJ could take my lead. It wasn't one of my most patient mornings I'm not proud to say, but a quick redirect turned that volatile situation around.

MORNING MADNESS

School mornings were often our most hectic time. Before I realised the importance of organisation, I just tried to 'wing it' usually resulting in what can only be described as 'morning madness'. Mornings can be difficult for any child, let alone when they're also naturally distractible, impulsive and hyperactive. To avoid delays and make mornings easier, it's great to have a routine set out for all of our children, not just our ADHD children.

Have a set list of what's expected and a time-frame. Let your children have some input. Put it in a prominent place so they can follow it and keep on track. This was ours below, and it worked when we stuck to it, especially the 'TV only if ready' part. (So, no more socks-on-hands debacles.) As my children grew older, I even had them make their beds as a part of their morning routine. It didn't have to be hospital corners; they just had to make an effort.

MORNING ROUTINE

- Out of bed 7 am;
- Five-minute shower, wet towels put in the laundry;
- Dressed & out of the bedroom by 7.30 am;
- Breakfast by 7.45 am;
- Check schoolbag/lunch/homework/notes;

- Make bed;
- Clean teeth;
- If ready, you can watch TV;
- Leave at 8.30 am for school; and,
- Kiss your mum.

CJ and Shari liked that they knew what to do and I didn't have to remind them (nag them) too much. All that was needed was a quick, "What are you supposed to be doing now?" and they could check for themselves. It also encouraged their time-telling and time-management skills. Initially, I was against allowing TV before school, but anything that kept CJ out of trouble in the morning was okay if he was ready. And always throw in that kiss for mum.

As well as having our morning routine, I found if I just did three things the night before, it made a huge difference to the stress level of the next morning:

- Lunches were planned and where possible prepared.
- Clothes from socks and shoes to jumpers and hair ties would be laid out ready.
- Homework, notes or money were packed in school bags.

You may already do this, but if not start now and feel the difference right from when you wake up. Tailor an age-dependent morning routine to suit your family. Keep it simple and stick with it to create helpful habits. Get up before the kids, get dressed and ready to deal with whatever comes your way for that whirlwind hour and a half in the morning.

DINNER TIME RUSH

Another testing time was the dinnertime rush. After a busy day at work, I'd be trying to cook dinner, and seven-year-old CJ would race around the house, mess up his toys, tease his sister and turn into tiny terror. I would constantly have to stop what I was doing just to check on him. I knew it was mostly for attention, but it was at a time when I couldn't give him this attention… or could I?

After some thought, I decided to ask him to help me with the cooking, not as a punishment but as a treat. He thought this was an excellent idea and was only too happy to assist me. Admittedly there was a little more mess, and he had some ideas of his own as to what we might have for dinner, but there was no longer that stress that had once been there. It also taught him a bit of responsibility, and a bit about cooking. It also provided an opportunity for us to spend some time together. Sometimes we forget that what is mundane to us can be a lot of fun to our kids.

BEDTIME BLUES

CJ was never tired early, but there was always a set

bedtime, so he knew well in advance when that time was. It was baby brother Harry to bed first, then Shari, then CJ. He was allowed an extra half hour which helped to make him feel that little bit special. It also helped me as I had time to read Shari her storybook, then I could concentrate on CJ. It's wasn't 'anything-goes' extra time, but wind-down time; peaceful and quiet in anticipation of sleep, having already bathed and put on pyjamas. I had to remind his dad though that the last half an hour wasn't the time for a mini world championship wrestling match. Rough and tumble before bed is like throwing the cat into the bath water and expecting it just to stroll casually away. Not going to happen!

Once in bed, even after his bedtime story, CJ was still often restless. I knew it was hard for him to lay there awake, trying to sleep when he didn't feel tired. If I tried to force him to sleep, it became a battle, so he was allowed a nightlight on. He could also have a book to read, a small toy to fiddle with, or a squishy stress ball to squeeze as he prepared to sleep.

There was to be no getting out of bed, and these things were usually enough to keep him quiet, but not enough to over-stimulate. I was happy for him to do this as long as he didn't get up. The limit was a half hour maximum, then night light off. He was usually good about this as he felt he was getting that little bit extra. The exceptions to this were Friday and Saturday nights, which were family movie night or games nights, so CJ knew he would get to stay up late if he played by the rules during the week.

TAKING THE BAIT

Tantrums are usually put on solely for our benefit. Once our attention is no longer given, there's no incentive to continue the behaviour. To our ADHD children, arguing is negotiating. The bigger an issue we make of it, the more we encourage them. Take away the opportunity, and eventually, they will get the message that you're in charge. Have your rules the way you want them to be. If a child pesters for more lollies or refuses to leave the playground, we might just give in because it's easier, but they soon learn that if they are loud enough and annoying enough, they'll eventually get their way. Tell them firmly how things are going to be. "That is all you are allowed for now." Then ignore their bad behaviour and continue on. Don't waver. Don't let them see that slight chink in your armour. They're clever and will pick up on this quickly, using it to their advantage. If it's at home, leave the room and take away your attention. If it's in public, remove them from the situation without a fuss. Take their hand or pick them up (maybe not your five foot tall, twelve-year-old!) and talk to them privately without an audience of any other parents or children. The bigger the audience, the bigger the show.

'NO'S AND WANTS

Like a red rag to a bull so is the word 'no' to the challenging child. To save sanity, try an option from the following menu in lieu of an outright 'no':

- "Not right now."
- "Maybe next time."
- "I'll think about it."
- "Hmm, good question."
- "I'm not too sure."
- "Ask your Dad."
- "Ask your Mum."
- "Let's talk about that later."
- "I'll keep that in mind."

Also keeping in mind that in the next hour there will be a dozen more requests and the current one will be long forgotten. (A useful reassurance for the stressed parent!) Angry bull averted unless, of course, the answer was 'yes'!

In our busy lives, we often just say 'no' to our children's requests without really thinking about it. Though we can't always say 'yes,' we can be the creators of many tricky times and problem situations just by overusing the word 'no'. We carelessly respond to many of our children's requests with a 'blanket no' and then wonder why they say 'no' to us so often.

It's often our immediate reaction, said without thinking or considering their request. Most of us don't like being told 'no' (unless of course, the question is 'Does my bum look big in this?'), and neither do our children. I would often find myself saying 'no' to CJ without actually listening, either because there seemed to be so many things that he wanted, or just because I was busy doing something else. He would then respond with "Not fair" or "Why not?" or "You always say no!"

I realised one day that I probably did. I realised that a few moments spent listening could save time and maybe an argument. When faced with yet another of their never-ending requests, ask yourself: Is there a compromise? Can we negotiate? Can we use this request in our favour, and also teach our child important skills at the same time?

He might ask, "Mum, can I have some ice-cream?" when he's supposed to be doing homework.

What I would usually say is, "No, you've got homework to get done

What I could also say is, "Sure you can, as soon as you finish your homework. I think you'll deserve that when you're done".

Which response can we predict will get the better result?

I would often use the 'blanket no' because I was annoyed about something. It would look like this:

CJ: "Can I go outside to play with Jack?"
Me: "No way. You've left Lego all over the floor."

Immediately—in our house anyway—we would have a conflict situation. Instead, I could have said, "Yes, that's fine. Just quickly tidy up that Lego, sweetheart. Thank you".

They may not completely like that reply, but it wasn't the standard 'no' and was more likely to get a better response (as well as getting the Lego off the floor!).

Maybe you're in the middle of a phone call (they always seem to ask when we're on the phone!) and he asks to go to the shop with some friends. You don't know any details and you don't have the time to ask. Rather than just saying 'no,' you could give a more diplomatic reply, such as, "I'll think about that, and I'll let you know in a few minutes when I'm off the phone, honey." Said nicely, with not a yes or a no in sight, but it will usually suffice.

CONSIDER A COMPROMISE

Ever hungry, CJ once asked me if he could have a chocolate biscuit right at bedtime. I said 'no' very definitely, so he asked for a sandwich, 'no,' "well a cracker then?" he persisted. I was becoming more impatient. "No!" I repeated. Then it occurred to me that he was, in his own way, doing what I was always trying to teach him. He was trying to compromise. I realised this was a positive thing, so I then said, "Okay. If you're really hungry, you can have a cracker". If he'd asked for the cracker in the first place, I probably would have said yes anyway!

At the toy shop, your child sees a cool robot with voice recognition. "Wow, can I get that? I want that, please? Why not? I want it!" And so goes the broken record.

Replace the 'no' with "Oh, wow. That's cool! You can save up for it if you like!" This gives the feeling of hope and possibility, and they will feel that they have been acknowledged, lessening the chance of a tantrum. Our children ask for a lot, but don't really expect to get it. They'll probably have forgotten the cool robot by the time you get to the next shop, and if not, it's now up to them start saving. If the answer is really a definite 'no,' explain calmly where possible, for example, "No, we can't go to the park, your Nanna will be here soon."

And there are those times that 'no' doesn't need any explanation. For instance, "I'm going to hit Lucy with this piece of wood."

"No. You are not," as Mum takes said big piece of wood from him.

It can be a revelation to count how many times a day we say 'no' to our kids or to our partners. Next time the blanket 'no' rears its head, see if you can replace it with a compromise. The result may surprise you. We often think that if we don't say 'no', it means we're weak, but in fact, it is the opposite. Just saying 'no' without any consideration can be like issuing a challenge to an already challenging child. Always consider a request for that few extra seconds and contemplate your response to gain a better outcome.

Do we want our kids to remember how 'no' was the standard answer, or rather how anything seemed possible by often hearing 'yes'? Keeping our 'no's for the more important things will make them more powerful, and in return, hopefully, lessen the amount of 'no's we get from our children.

These are just some examples of the testing times we may have with our children. Expect them, plan for them and adjust for them. Sometimes our kids are just tired and grumpy. Often we are too. But we will also have good times, great times and exceptional times. These are the times that make everything worthwhile.

TRAVEL TIPS:

- Change the scenery to change the mood.
- Have a consistent routine, adjust when needed.
- Consider compromise, rather than a 'no!'

14. TRIALS AND TRIBULATIONS

"The way we deal with a situation determines the outcome—we can ease or exacerbate, help or hinder, depending on our response."

As a preschooler, though distractible, excitable and often up to mischief, CJ seemed about as happy as any other child, and generally wanted to please. He didn't like to be in trouble but frequently found himself right in the middle of it without knowing why. He could be defiant, but usually, it didn't last for too long. For his age, it seemed not too far from the ordinary. I knew all children matured at their own pace and each brought different challenges. But when challenges don't lessen with time, maturity can seem like a faraway planet.

More complicated issues than 'who gets to sit in the front of the car' or 'who gets to choose the morning cartoon' will arise. New, more serious parenting minefields rise forth to be navigated through. As our children become older, they become more influenced by outside factors and our own influence is lessened. We may then have to deal with darker issues such as defiance, lying, volatile outbursts, swearing, or even stealing.

DEFLECTING DEFIANCE

Defiance became one of our major battles. CJ didn't like to be told what to do. He didn't like to be wrong. He didn't like to be told he was wrong. He didn't like to be sent to his room. He didn't like to be told 'no'. In a volatile or emotional situation, I often made the big mistake of trying to make CJ do something: "Right. That's it. Get those dishes done now," or "That's it. Go to your room. Yes, now". Considering it could be hard to make him do anything anytime, what was I thinking, trying to make him do something when he was at his most difficult? It was just adding stress to an already stressful situation.

He couldn't very well just do what I'd demanded; we were in battle, on opposite sides. He couldn't give in even if he wanted to. It would be letting down 'team CJ', and he had too much pride to let that happen. I came to see that I was a contributor to his non-cooperation; that I was making demands I knew he wouldn't adhere to. I knew him all too well.

To counteract this, I decided to stop trying to force him to do anything when he was in a difficult mood. I wouldn't become part of the war. I wouldn't create the stress of trying to force my already-stubborn son to go somewhere or to do something. Instead of sending him to that unforgiving jail-like place, aka his bedroom, I could give myself a break and give him a caution—a simple, "Please stop that now, that's not nice," or "I'll talk to you when you're more reasonable". I would then divert my attention away from him, not giving him any more. In doing so, I could cease to be a contributing factor to his defiance, and instead become a positive factor toward a more peaceful solution.

TALL TALES

One of the biggest parenting mistakes I made was punishing CJ when he told the truth. If asked, "Did you hit your sister?" or" Did you swear at the teacher?" he would say, "Yes, I did!" And then I would punish him. I'd get the truth first and then send him to his room or "No TV tonight". He soon realised that if he told me the truth, he'd most likely be punished. It wasn't until much later I realised my error. I was teaching him to lie. My fault. A rookie parenting mistake. He soon figured out that to avoid punishment the answer was not to tell Mum anything! Just deny, deny and deny!

I should have been using his truthfulness as an opportunity to correct wrong behaviours. A thank you for your honesty and let's talk about what happened and why; an explanation from CJ and some understanding from me thrown in.

Our kids learn to lie to keep themselves out of trouble. If telling the truth hasn't been a positive experience in the past, they'll try to give us what they think we want to hear. It then becomes a habit, and they lie about things that don't even matter before they even realise. Being protective of themselves, they're not about to admit to wrongdoing if they can help it. If we say, "You're lying!" then they'll just deny. After all, we don't have an actual lie detector machine, they don't have to go before a judge, and there are no hidden cameras to 100% prove them wrong.

Rather than trying to force a confession, (somewhat like trying to force an elephant through your front door) try a more gentle approach. "Hmm, that doesn't sound exactly right," or "I don't think so. Have a think about it and try again". Tell them it's okay, we get things mixed up too sometimes. Give them a few minutes to revise their story. Alternatively, if a lie is plainly evident, there's always that look that we can give, that double chinned frown that says, 'I don't believe you, but I'm not going to bother because we both know it'. The best thing to do is to make it okay to tell the truth, no punishing for telling the truth, but an appreciation of it being given, even in a bad circumstance.

Other times our children can lie to impress with silly things that are more exaggerations than lies; such as a fisherman's tale as to the size of their catch. How big did you say? Or it might be a conversation that you know would never actually happen in reality. It might go something like this: "And all the kids said that I was the best in the grade at everything". It might be facts that you know aren't true: "I looked up our family name, and we're related to a famous explorer!" You point out their name is spelt differently, and they respond, "I know! They changed the spelling". If it's a 'trying to impress' issue, then work with them on their self-esteem, so they feel good about themselves and have no need to make things up. If it's not important, shrug it off, or use 'the look' with a smile. They'll get the point. We all tell little white lies at some point, don't we? "I didn't realise you called. Sorry! My phone was on silent," or "Oh, wow. Bleached blonde really suits you!"

UNFORGIVING TIMES

Our ADHD kids live very much in the here and now, once something is done, that's it, finished, and they can't figure out why they are still in trouble later. It can be hard to be nice to our children after an issue or confrontation. One frazzled mum told me that she found it hard to forgive her son after a stressful confrontation. She would pull away from him when he reached out afterward as if nothing had happened. We can make an effort to practise forgiveness rather than resentment even at the most difficult or exasperating of times, keeping in mind that ADHD is a contributing factor to their behaviour. Our kids didn't ask for it, but it's there regardless. When they yell, "I hate you," it really means "I'm hurt and frustrated". Though we too are hurt and frustrated, don't take their words too personally.

CJ was often hungry late in the day due to Ritalin lessening his appetite. To save arguments over this (or so I thought), we had a rule that the kitchen 'closed' at 7.30 pm and he could have something to eat up until that time. One night at 7.20 pm, CJ informed me that he was 'starving'. I told him if he was quick he could have a bowl of cereal or a sandwich. Sounds fair, right? Well, he decided that he wanted to cook pasta, so of course, I said no. He then began to demand, "Why not?" repeatedly yelling that I was starving him. I said firmly, "I'm sorry, CJ, it's too late. Eat something that doesn't need cooking". He then began to yell, as loud as his little lungs could muster, that I hated him and I was a bad mother, and that he may as well run away and live somewhere where they will feed him better.

Through gritted teeth, I told him to go outside for a few minutes in the fresh air to calm down. It was a warm summer night, and surprisingly he complied without protest. But within minutes he began to kick the glass sliding door while continuing to yell about the injustice of not being given any food. God only knows what the neighbours were thinking! I brought him back inside and asked him to be quiet. With that, he yelled again that I was starving him and that he deserved a better mother and that he wanted to punch me in the face and kill me (just what every mother wants to hear!) He added that he would have to kill his dad too because if he didn't, his dad would probably kill him (that was certainly the most reasonable thought process he'd had in the last ten minutes). He was getting even more worked up, so I told him to have his shower and pondered how we got from pasta to murder in a few crazy minutes? I wasn't happy. Fortunately, though, I kept my calm and hadn't mirrored CJ's temperament. I knew he loved his hot showers, so hopefully, the water had washed off not only the dirt but his bad mood as well. Strangely it had.

Out of the shower, he acted as if nothing had happened and he asked for the bowl of cereal telling me that was all he really wanted in the first place. Short memory. After his cereal, he was told it would be bedtime for him. He asked his dad why he couldn't stay up to watch TV. (Yes, he did need to ask because he would quickly forget the things he'd said.) Angrily he then trudged to his room, and when I went to talk to him, he told me it was my fault he was in trouble because I had told his dad. I looked at him and shook my head with the double-chinned frown pose that he knew so well. Then I left his room without a word to hopefully give him time to think about the silly circus we'd just had.

I went back about ten minutes later deliberately saying nothing of the pasta commotion. He seemed relieved. I sat on his bed and asked if he had anything to say. He shook his head. So, quietly, I said, "I was really hurt when you said you wanted to kill me".

He replied, "I don't really. I just got angry".

"Please try to think more about what you say

when you're angry."

"Okay, sorry. I'll be better tomorrow". That wasn't easy for him, but apology accepted. It had opened the door for a rational discussion.

"You said you wanted a mum that loves you, well, you have one. Do you know what parents are for?" I asked him

"To tell us what to do?" he replied.

"Well, yes, at times, but more to teach you and keep you safe. So, if I tell you something you can always ask why, but I expect you to do as I ask."

"Okay," he said, maybe grudgingly, but he listened and didn't argue. I'll take that. I gave him a big hug.

"See you in the morning. I love you."

"I love you too," he said with an apologetic half-smile.

There was no lecture, no threat, and no crazy mum threatening to lock him in his room for all eternity (for a change!). It was just an open talk without grudges and a little forgiveness thrown in. Many parents would say, shut him in his room, he deserves it, don't give in; but teaching a child forgiveness isn't giving in. Both he and I could go to sleep with a bad situation resolved and start fresh the next day. Even now, reading this, it sounds crazy, (and he never ever punched me in the face!) but there will be crazy times when our ADHD children experience that loss of control. The best thing we can do is to not 'get crazy' with them.

BATTLE CHOICES

It's important for us to pick our battles and ask ourselves 'is the argument worth the cost'.

There was a school excursion to the historical ship, now a tourist attraction, The Polly Woodside. Being a late return home, it would have meant that CJ might miss out on his basketball game that night. It was also on the same day as his regular after-school skateboarding meet. All week he sulked and complained about the excursion insisting that it wasn't fair, and I was making him go. It was getting on my nerves, so I thought about how it would affect his life if he didn't go and decided that it wouldn't really make any difference. I was sure that he would enjoy seeing the Polly Woodside with his dad being a seafaring person, but he complained so much that it simply wasn't worth the argument. So, I told CJ, "You don't have to go; I'll leave it up to you".

"Good, I don't want to go," he replied

"Okay, that's fine. I'll let the teacher know." He looked a little surprised and even then, I could tell he was having second thoughts. Later he asked hesitantly, "Do you really want me to go on the excursion?"

Again, I said, "It's totally up to you".

A short while later he decided to go on the excursion. He called his skateboard pal and arranged to go skateboarding another day. He had a great time and still made it home for basketball.

The more we disagree with our ADHD children, the more they will disagree with us. If it's not vital that they do something, let them decide for themselves. They might just surprise you. They won't resent you for forcing them, and they will feel a little proud that they were allowed to make their own decision. If CJ hadn't gone on the excursion, he might have regretted his decision when he heard the other children talking about what a great time they had, and then hopefully make the right choice next time. If not, no harm done as an extra day at school doesn't go astray.

PUNCH HAPPY

For a time, CJ would punch his sister constantly. Not hard, but often and for the smallest irritation. She may have talked while he was talking, taken his spoon, or sat in 'his chair' (this incidentally seemed to be every chair). If punished, he would only want to hit her harder the next time because to him it was Shari's fault that he was in trouble. The only way I could get him to see how his behaviour affected her (and no, not by punching him back!) was by giving him examples and asking questions, such as, "If you sit in my seat, do you think I should punch you?"

When he replied, "No," I would ask why not, and he would tell me that he didn't want to be punched and he hadn't done anything wrong. I would say well your sister feels the same way, then ask him what the difference was. Obviously, there was none. I explained that it's okay to feel angry, but he can come and tell me of the great injustice done. I'd listen, and we could talk about alternatives. He said he did it usually without thinking, so I asked him to try hard to think about it first. Then think about how it would feel to not be in trouble.

I knew that being so easily frustrated he needed an outlet for his anger, so we drew a grumpy face (no not mine!) on an old pillow and called it the punching-pillow. Anytime the 'angry punching monsters' wanted to come out, I'd hold the pillow for him to punch out his frustration. It came to be fun for CJ to ask for the punching pillow and he would usually end up laughing with Shari adding a punch or two in as well. Rather than just being 'told off' we can help kids to be more aware and find better ways to deal with their feelings.

LANGUAGE LAWS

In today's world, language standards have dropped. Our children hear swear words at school, at times from their parents, in movies and even on the radio. Some children feel that swearing makes them cool or tough, stronger or scarier. The best thing we can do today is to set the example, to not swear ourselves; to let them know that it is unacceptable and stick to it. Again, a harsh, angry reaction from us probably won't work, as they will most likely be swearing at you under your breath when you've finished. As time went on, swearing became an issue for us with CJ. It seemed appealing to convey his anger and frustration in that way.

He did make an effort to not swear in front of me, but I still wasn't' happy for him to swear anywhere, whether I heard it or not. He knew the rules. They were simple. No swearing allowed or there would be consequences. Depending on the severity, it might have been a $2 fine, miss out on seeing a movie, lose his video game for the day, or whatever hit the spot at that time. At one point, CJ was losing almost all his pocket money in swearing fines, so eventually this habit was curbed, for a while anyway. I would also tell CJ that using those words made it look like you're not smart enough to think of the proper words for the occasion. It worked briefly.

Often, our kids have no idea what a word actually means, and I had to be blunt and tell CJ, in a child-suitable way, the meaning of a certain four-letter word he'd decided to use. He was horrified to find out what he was really saying (well, briefly anyway). I tried to teach him to use different words. We'd get the thesaurus and have a bit of fun and make it a learning experience. It worked, also briefly. If CJ hadn't been swearing, I'd comment on how pleased I was with him. He may have been swearing outside the home, but I'd let his conscience deal with that. Eventually, it would have to anyway. We're kidding ourselves to think our children won't ever swear, but we can give them standards to aspire to by not swearing either. (And paying the same $2 fine as they do, if we do!)

Light Fingers

We were fortunate to have no issue with CJ stealing. Some other parents aren't so lucky. It's important to look at why kids are stealing. Is it because they need something? Or because it makes them feel cool? Is it to impress friends? Knowing the motivations helps us to work on the remedy. If it's to impress friends or seems to be for no particular reason, then it may be more their self-esteem that needs work.

One mum at our ADHD group told me of her son's problem with stealing. She also added that he was never given pocket money due to his bad behaviour. Here was the classic catch-22 situation. No money to buy anything, so he steals. As a result of stealing, he doesn't receive any pocket money.

If this is an issue with your child, tell them that you're worried. Explain that you are concerned about their future. No one likes a thief, and thieves can end up in jail. Let them know if they need something they should tell you. If they want something, they can make these *wants* into *goals* and plan for them by starting a money box or putting on a layby. Possibly they can earn extra pocket money by helping more at home. When they see what they can achieve by being honest, they'll gain that sense of accomplishment which will guide them toward more constructive ways of acquiring the things they want.

FIRE FASCINATION

CJ was extremely fascinated by fire. Of course, 'paranoid me' worried that he would try to make his own version of a campfire in the backyard when we weren't around, with toy blocks and tree bark.

To satisfy his fiery desires, he was allowed help to light any fire that we were having at home. It might have been a bonfire of old wood and papers outside, or the slow combustion fire in his dad's shed to keep warm in winter. He loved to watch the flames, and we would make it a family event with marshmallows on sticks.

The dangers were explained to him in the normal course of a conversation, so it didn't feel like a lecture. We'd talk about what we could safely burn and what we could not, how the weather conditions needed to be to safely burn-off outside, and that fires were only appropriate when an adult was present. He gained a healthy respect for fire, knowing the dangers and how quickly it could cause damage and injury. He was proud to be allowed to help with any fire-lighting and appreciated the trust we had given him.

These are just some of the trials and tribulations that may arise. As one issue diminishes, a new one pokes out its pesky head, ready to take its rightful place. We can only take them as they come, day to day, sometimes minute to minute. We can prepare for them where possible. We can acknowledge them and find answers through better communication. We often try to fix things for our children without asking them for input. They're smarter than they seem. They know more than we give them credit for and often in trusting them to be part of their own solutions, we will find our resolutions.

TRAVEL TIPS:

- Weigh the cost and pick your battles.
- Contribute to the solution, not the problem.
- Communicate, acknowledge, resolve.

15. YOUR CHILD'S SELF-ESTEEM

"The foundations of self-esteem are built during childhood with parents the chief engineers."

Before the ADHD diagnosis, CJ's self-esteem had plummeted. He had begun to hide his beautiful, unique personality for fear of rejection and from constantly being in trouble. He'd begun to put up a tough, defiant façade as a self-protective barrier from those around him. That often included me. After the diagnosis, and armed with my new-found knowledge, it was time to help him regain some of this lost self-esteem; time to repair the damage done to his outlook on life. He would need encouragement to be himself again, and more importantly to like himself again.

Even though our ADHD children can be loud and excitable with seemingly not a care in the world, they can also be depressed for no apparent reason. Often, they won't talk about it because they don't know exactly how to put that feeling into words. It could be, as it was often in CJ's mind, the overwhelming sense that 'nothing I do is right' and 'everybody hates me'. Just saying 'cheer up' won't do much, or worse, telling them to 'stop sulking' will just make them feel that someone else is annoyed with them, another burden to add to their little emotional backpack.

Instead, we can ask how we can help, then listen carefully and think constructively toward finding a solution. Sometimes there isn't one. We can still be there with reassurance, a hug and our attention. Often, it's more our child's perception of something rather than the actual event that may be the problem. Our children's perceptions can be very different to the perceptions of those around them, including our own. We shouldn't just assume their perception of an event is wrong just because it's different, but we can become mini-investigators to understand their view and discuss the differences.

ALTERING PERCEPTIONS

CJ was chosen to participate in a science fair. I was thrilled for him, but his immediate response was an angry, "No way. I'm not doing that!"

I was annoyed. Here we go again, I thought dejectedly. Instead of seeing a great opportunity he viewed it as some sort of punishment. My excitement was met with sulking and defiance. Here was a chance to be part of a hand-picked group and show his science talents.

It should have been a time for us to be proud of him, but he was insistent that he wouldn't be doing it. 'He's letting us down again,' I thought, but then it occurred to me that I hadn't taken the time to ask him why he didn't want to do it. I'd just been telling him that he should do it, that he was missing a good opportunity and how we would be disappointed if he didn't do it. It was all about what *I* thought, and I hadn't really delved any further into what *he* was thinking.

Later that day, we sat down for ice-cream so I subtly I used this 'happy ice-cream moment' to slot in the subject of the science competition. He immediately became downcast. I told him I wasn't going to force him to do it, but asked him why he didn't want to. To ask this question hadn't even occurred to me earlier. His simple answer surprised me. He replied, "Because I'll look stupid". My heart melted. He wasn't 'not participating' because he was lazy or couldn't be bothered. He was just worried that he wasn't good enough. That also hadn't occurred to me. After a big hug, I explained to him that he was chosen because his teachers thought that he was definitely good enough and that it was also meant to be fun. I added that the other children probably were as worried as he was. With a little more positive reinforcement he decided later that he would participate, and he did just fine. Poor self-esteem can be a barrier to opportunities for a child to improve their self-esteem. Another child's perception might have been 'I must be good to be chosen,' and it would have been a boost to their self-esteem, but CJ's perception was that it was another thing to fail at, and, therefore, another thing to avoid.

Take the following example:
Our boss is great. He's hardly ever in, and he leaves the decisions to us. He trusts us completely.

Compared to:
Our boss is lousy. He's hardly ever in, and we're expected to make all the decisions. He's just plain lazy. We can't depend on him.

Same boss, same workplace, but totally opposing perceptions; so, who is right? Both may be right. Each has a similar experience, but their perception of it depends on a person's individual viewpoint. It can be a revelation to find out how things look from our child's perspective when we dig that little bit deeper.

Upon understanding how our child views themselves, we can help to alter false perceptions when we take the time to ask the right questions and try to see what a child sees. We can be on their side by trying to understand their thought process and motives. If you can't fully be on their side, don't be the enemy. At the very least be Switzerland and stay neutral. A child will more readily accept another viewpoint when situations are explained with understanding by someone that they trust. Acknowledge their feelings and help them to see another viewpoint that may never have occurred to them on their own. In turn, we may see a new viewpoint from our child that may never have occurred to us. Win-win.

DO THEY KNOW?

We often take it for granted that our kids just know what is expected or what to do in everyday situations, so we overlook the basics. They can't know what they *don't yet* know. We can damage their self-confidence by scolding them for things that seem common sense to us.

CJ, along with his sister, loved to help with the baking One day he asked if he could bake a cake all by himself (under my supervision). I'd watched as he'd carefully mixed together his ingredients, but as I looked to check the oven temperature, he poured his cake mix into the unbuttered (and not non-stick) baking pan. My first impulse was a feeling of irritation, and I went to point out his error; but then I realised that I'd never really told him about lining or buttering a cake pan. Rather than my initial impulse which would have just made him feel bad, I said, "Oh, CJ. I'm sorry. I haven't told you about buttering the pan". I then went on to explain how to do that. He accepted my 'apology' with his self-esteem intact rather than him thinking that he'd 'messed up' yet again. We went on to move the mixture into a prepared cake pan with no harm done.

KIND WORDS—KIND HEARTS

With the hectic pace of life and challenges that come

with ADHD, we can spend a lot of our words on correcting and criticising, groaning and grumbling. Ensure you don't unwittingly contribute to damaging your child's opinion of themselves. We all know the adage 'sticks and stones may break my bones, but names will never hurt me', but this isn't always true. Words can hurt much more to sensitive souls. Physical ailments heal, but young minds can hold onto the adverse effects of our words, and these hurts may never fully heal. Words that are like 'water off a duck's back' to other children will stick like glue with ours.

We can find ourselves making offhand comments, such as, "You're such a silly boy Tom," or "Yes, Will's our little trouble-maker," or "Oh, Kate, you're always breaking something".

Our children will ultimately believe what we tell them about themselves. These beliefs come through in both our words, and our attitude, and can become accepted by them as 'who they are'.

We take for granted that our children know how we feel about them, but it's important to find something genuine to praise them for every day. It doesn't have to be anything over the top, but try to notice little things that they do. A simple, "Oh, you're ready early. That's great!" with a smile as you walk past, will give them that little boost—another deposit in their self-esteem bank. You don't have to go overboard, just be genuine. "Well done, your room looks good," or a simple, "Thanks. Good job, mate," are small things to say that make a huge difference in letting your child know they've done well. In turn, they'll feel pleased with themselves.

Don't leave kind words just for days when they're feeling a bit down. A regular supply of subtle praise will lift their spirits and is more beneficial than any monetary reward (or chocolate!) in the long term. Maybe Kate does break a few things, or Tom can be a 'silly boy' but don't let past mistakes colour your outlook and become their identity.

PRECONCEPTIONS

I was quite protective of CJ, and being a worrier, I liked to go on school excursions so I could watch out for him. On one particular excursion, there was a boy called Mathew also in CJ's Grade 4 class. Getting off the bus, one of the teachers pointed to him, and with a stern don't-mess-around look, said sharply, "You'd better behave, Mathew, or you'll sit on the bus all day!" Obviously, he was considered 'one of the naughty kids' and the teacher wasn't going to forget this. Immediately, his expression changed, a frown replacing the excited look of moments before.

I felt for him. It was exactly what I imagined happening to CJ in my absence. As it turned out, Mathew was in my group, so I embraced the opportunity.

"Hi, Matthew. You're with me today," I said in a friendly voice. He looked at me warily and nodded.

During the morning, I purposely made an effort to engage him in conversation and treat him as nicely as any other child. I chatted about the scenery and asked simple questions about his likes and hobbies. Slowly he responded, and by mid-morning he was happily making conversation back. I had no trouble with him during the excursion, and it was a good day. It was heart-warming how just a little effort brought about a positive change from Mathew's morning demeanour.

We said goodbye, and he headed for the back seat of the bus while I sat near the front with CJ. As we were about to leave, there was a commotion from the back. Without any hesitation, a teacher's voice boomed. "Mathew! You can come and sit up here with me." (Blame the usual instigator and don't ask any questions!) And off he trudged to the front of the bus.

I felt disappointed for him that such a positive day had ended up, clearly the same as most others did; and that Mathew seemed quite resigned to this 'naughty kid' label. Maybe he was the instigator, maybe not, but it seemed he had been defined as the usual suspect and had no trouble living up to this expectation. With the teacher using what she considered a preventative warning, she was setting the scene for more of the same problem. Children usually come to do what they think we expect of them even if it's misbehaving!

Instead, they can be given more positive

reinforcement, in anticipation of trust even when they might not entirely deserve it. A little kindness even on a bad day makes a huge difference to their spirits as well as their choices and the outcomes of those choices.

FRIENDS IN ONE BASKET

Self-esteem is tied into so many different aspects, eventually becoming very much tied to our children's friendships and social interactions. I found that with CJ and friendships, it was important to have a choice and not just rely on one relationship. A child doesn't have to have one best friend. If they do they're lucky, but if that suddenly changes a child can end up feeling lost and left out. It can be a massive withdrawal from the self-esteem bank, so it's wise to encourage a variety of friendships.

CJ used to play with two brothers that lived across the road. This seemed perfect, but then a new boy, Brady moved to the street. The brothers began to play more with Brady instead, and CJ often felt excluded. Of course, this upset him very much. He would watch from the window and ask why his friends didn't like him anymore. When Brady wasn't around, the brothers would come to play, and all would seem well with the world. But it was never long before Brady was back on the scene and CJ would be left on his own. He became sullen, hurt and angry. These negative feelings began to make life unpleasant, not just for CJ, but for all of us. It was time to give him a little assistance. I decided that any child that he'd played with at school, for even the smallest amount of time would be invited over.

About eight different boys, some from CJ's class but also some a little younger, were invited over at different times and initially for short visits. Most of the mums were more than happy to have a break for a few hours, so it was no problem getting these prospective friends to come over. Naturally, some of them didn't work out, but a few did, and because we were so eager to have them visit, they became good friends of CJ. As he made these new friends, it was evident that the issue with the boys in our street had become less important to his happiness and self-esteem. Soon he didn't really mind whether he saw them or not. When he did, there was no animosity, and he had new things to talk to them about. In turn, he became more interesting to them, and they all ended up playing together again.

Sometimes we need to lend a hand to the friend-making process to start them off, but it's well worth it in the long term. If all else fails and you have a disheartened child with no friend on the horizon for a play date, actively include them in your day. Subtly cheer them up by keeping them too busy to dwell on it: "I'd love some help to bake these cookies please!" Or change the environment to change the mood. "Let's go to the library, or let's take Patch for a walk." Keep in mind that a pet can be the perfect friend, and a great self-esteem booster.

KEEPING BUSY

Hobbies and sports are a great way to boost your child's self-esteem and is also another avenue for making new friends and gaining new interests. CJ tried a variety. Not everything suited but he gave most of them a good go. He went to Cub Scouts which interested him at first, but he began to have trouble with some of the other boys. He tried guitar lessons and karate, but his poor coordination put him off. He loved fishing and boating with his dad and still does to this day.

If you have a favourite activity, get them interested as well. Children often do things because a parent does and come to love it just as much.

High energy team sports are also great, like football and basketball. It's a great experience for our children to work as a team alongside others, winning and losing and following rules. Become involved where you can. Be the goalie, work in the canteen. Watch them practise. Encourage them to keep going if their first few attempts don't go as planned. If they're not overly confident, practise with them. Do it as a family; take the cricket set or footy to the local oval to build up their confidence, or play a game in the backyard. A basketball hoop at home can be lots of fun for parents too! It will help them to practise taking turns, sharing and teach them fair play. There may be some conflict moments, but better to learn the rules at home before tackling the real deal.

Give them input as to what they would like and try anything they seem interested in where possible. Be open to new things and be spontaneous. CJ mentioned once that he wanted to try squash, so I booked us a game together at the local sports centre. We had no idea what we were doing, but we had the racquets and the ball, and a lot of fun trying to figure it out.

If they like to dance or sing, paint, draw or even cook give them the opportunity to try out a class. Ensure they persist. One class alone isn't enough to gauge their interest. I remember CJ's first basketball game well. Each time he made a mistake he put his hand over his face in embarrassment (no, you can't just disappear!). He didn't want to go back at first, but the deal was if he signed up he had to stay for the term. No dropping out after one try. It didn't look like this would end well, but by the end of his first season he'd vastly improved and won 13 points out of 25 in their last game. Though they didn't win that game, CJ walked away proud.

ADHD AND MEDICATION

The diagnosis of ADHD can contribute to a child's low self-esteem. It's up to us to show them it's not a bad thing, just a different thing. It's not something they've done or to be ashamed of. Help your child to accept their ADHD by giving other examples of disorders requiring medications such as epilepsy, asthma and diabetes. Other children may need glasses, a hearing aid or wheelchair. It is up to us to encourage a positive attitude around medication.

As well as ADHD, CJ also had asthma and severe eczema. Both required medication and CJ knew well the benefits of using them. When it came for him to take his ADHD medication, I explained in a way I thought he could understand using his other ailments as a comparison. I told him that in his brain, his on and off, fast and slow buttons weren't always working properly and that's why he often found himself in trouble. Just like the car accelerator stuck on full speed ahead with faulty brakes will inevitably crash. I explained that his Ritalin was a medicine, just like his Ventolin for his asthma. Ritalin would help control these functions in his brain more effectively and would help him to better control his impulses, to avoid distractions and stay focused. For CJ this was a good explanation and one he could comprehend; one that he could see the benefit of and feel good about himself.

Our role is to give our children a stable, loving environment and a safe haven from the daunting 'big world'. They need our guidance, trust and support, to feel loved for who they are, rather than who society expects them to be. We can appreciate a child's efforts regardless of the end result. We can praise not only the large successes, but also their smaller victories. It's these small victories that will add up in time to form their overall success and feeling of self-worth. People with good self-esteem are happy people and isn't that the ultimate goal we have for our children.

TRAVEL TIPS:

- Look from your child's eyes to gain a new perspective.
- Contribute regularly to their self-esteem bank.
- Steer them in the right direction with friends and hobbies.

16. SCHOOLING—A TEAM EFFORT

"Teacher—a parent's support and a vital ally, to whom the baton is passed each school day."

Our child's education can be one of our biggest challenges. We want our child to thrive, to fit in and to be happy. After so much silliness with CJ's early childhood behaviour, and my 'first-child-fumble-through' style of parenting, I had high hopes for this new phase of his life—his school life.

Prior to CJ starting primary school, I hadn't heard of Attention Deficit Hyperactivity Disorder, so I just assumed that his excitable behaviour was due to that fact that I was a first-time parent finding my way. I thought that the restriction and routine of a school class would be exactly what he needed. I knew that he was intelligent and was certain this would shine through when he began school life, like a hidden child genius emerging (the clouds would part, the heavens would open, and the sun would shine down on this gifted child!). But I was wrong.

It was hard; hard to see him heading off eagerly to school so excited, then within a few weeks to have him crying in the car, begging me not to send him in. I would walk him into class clutching his hand tightly. When I'd let go, he would run and hide under the table with the teacher looking at me impatiently as if

I had brought a mischievous chipmunk into the class. My feelings of sadness and compassion for CJ soon became overridden by my embarrassment and feelings of failure as a parent at this basic part of life, sending my child to school. It was yet another flat tyre on the bumpy road of parenthood.

Ideally, our ADHD children will be in a small class in a small school designed to meet their additional needs, with caring teachers well trained and experienced in this area (a violin plays and birds sing sweetly). But we don't live in a perfect world, so unless you are fortunate enough to find a suitable private school and be fortunate enough to be able to afford the fees, this is not what will happen.

WHICH SCHOOL? WHICH TEACHER?

Many ADHD children will go to a local public school and be expected to cope in mainstream education. While this may not be the perfect scenario, there are a few ways to ensure a good education for your child. Firstly, do your homework (pardon the pun!). It's easy to simply pick the closest school, but unless it's necessary for transportation or work reasons, look around.

Look at other possible school choices. Look online for information on your selected schools. Read their mission statement to gain an insight into their values. Ask friends, work colleagues and other parents in your area for their opinion of the schools that their children go to. Not that personal opinion is always an accurate measure, but it can be taken into consideration. Visit each school to ask about their policies and programs. Ask about their attitude toward various things such as welfare and discipline, and if they have a lot of experience with ADHD children.

I visited CJ's former primary school and spoke to the principal, who has set in place many strategies and programs for not only ADHD children, but for any child with additional needs. They have programs in place such as Kitchen Club where children get to use recipes and cook. They have a hands-on learning program for children that need more activity in their day.

For children with ADHD and additional requirements, they have team meetings to discuss the progress of children and have regular contact with parents. They try to ensure that ADHD children feel as welcome as any other child and are accommodated for their individual traits and idiosyncrasies. It might be they only like sitting on a certain chair or in a certain area, or having something small to fidget with, or even sitting in a tee-pee.

There's no longer such a stigma about ADHD, and it's best to be upfront and open about your child's strengths and weaknesses. There are bound to be some problems, and the more aware the teachers are, the better prepared they will be to help your child. After the ADHD diagnosis, I always asked that

CJ was placed in a grade with the teacher that was most happy to have him there. Some teachers can be more experienced or more successful with ADHD kids than others, and I always wanted them to have this choice. Regard your child's teacher as an ally. They'll need your back-up and support. Don't be intimidated. They are only people like us, and while this is part of their job; don't just expect it to be easy for them. If it's hard for us to manage at home, imagine how hard it can be for a teacher with another twenty-five children in the room.

EDUCATING THE TEACHER

You can *educate* the teacher without seeming pushy and use your mum/dad insider-knowledge to help them bring out the best in your child. Be prepared with a list of topics you'd like to discuss, sticking to the main points. If you're not feeling confident or you're not good with words, take someone to advocate for you—someone who knows your child well.

Your list should include your concerns, your expectations and your child's strong points and personality traits. No one knows your child better than you. I was probably the pain-in-the-butt mum with my suggestions and strategies, but I always went into a parent /teacher meeting with a good attitude and a positive manner, not presumptuously as if I didn't trust their methods, but as an added assistance.

Today, with so much awareness of ADHD, teachers will already have strategies in place, but you can also offer some of your own.

The following are a few tried and true methods for helping ADHD children excel in a classroom setting:

- Give concise instructions and specifically ask if the child knows what to do.
- If it's not written on the board, get the child to write it down to stay on task.
- Check regularly to make sure the child is keeping up with the class.
- Seat them away from distractions such as the door or window.
- The front of the class can be best for seating or with the quieter children
- CJ liked to sit with the girls, as they weren't so distracting (that changed later!).
- Give them responsibility even if they may not deserve it, for example, taking the lunch orders to the canteen or a message to the office. (We all do better when we feel important)
- If becoming disruptive, counter with a distraction. "CJ, can you help me with these worksheets please?" Often, it can be that simple.
- Motivate good behaviour by believing in them and expecting their best.
- Promote self-esteem with praise for effort not

just for the end result. They may be trying harder than others for a lesser result.

Always let the teacher know that their efforts are appreciated. They need validation too! It may seem like a lot of work, but it's really not. It's probably taken longer for me to write this for you (about twenty years in the making!) than it takes to have an informative chat with the teacher. After CJ's diagnosis, we were lucky for him to be placed the following year into a class with a teacher 'known for strictness' but also for consistency, Mrs Prescott. She set in place specific reminders for CJ if he was becoming rowdy or distractible so he would be aware before a problem arose. He wasn't' made to feel embarrassed, and it was just between them. This could be a subtle tap on his desk with a pen, or she might ask him to do a small task. He came to appreciate not being in trouble all the time and worked well in this class.

Talk to your child's teacher about using reminder cues if they don't already, such as the pencil tap on the desk before a situation arises. Another teacher used to put marbles in a cup. One marble meant 'a little off track', two meant 'uh oh, you need to settle down', three meant 'you need to come and see me'. The marbles could convey a message without drawing too much attention or embarrassment. Prevention is better than waiting for a problem to arise, and it can take only one small incident to send them off track.

We also set up a communication book, though now your school may prefer text or email communication. This book went back and forth from home to school, with daily issues addressed and worded in a respectful way. Any serious problems meant the book could be used to ask me to come in for a chat, with a brief reason so as not to embarrass CJ. Mrs Prescott also looked for the positives to comment on. Reading these comments to CJ had an encouraging impact on his self-esteem and his school life. Often there was even a gold star in the book when he had worked well. This helped CJ to see his progress, to stay on track and to feel good about school.

It's great to get that positive feedback, but there will always be some negative. If so, don't be disheartened; just use it as another starting point for improvement. Instead of saying resignedly, "I just don't know what to do with him," accept it as part of the ADHD parcel and ask, "What can we do to overcome or improve on this?" Work together as a team, brainstorming and continuing to try new strategies for a better educational outcome.

KEEP UP THE COMMUNICATION

Always let the teacher know if something's going on at home that may affect your child's school day. If they didn't get much sleep the night before, if

Grandma is sick or a pet has passed away, anything that might make them more sensitive or emotional. They can then be given that extra dose of understanding throughout the day.

I still have our old book. Here are some of the comments:

> **Teacher:** *CJ does not really know what 'quiet reading' is. He is not the only one, will have to have a reminder lesson.*
>
> **Me:** *I have had a talk with CJ and let him know how proud I would be if he can try his best to improve his behaviour at reading time. I have promised him an extra star sticker if I hear that he is trying to improve his behaviour at quiet reading time.*
>
> **Teacher:** *CJ had a quiet and productive quiet reading time, well done!*
>
> ********
>
> **Teacher:** *CJ wasn't very well-behaved during library today. Talkative when lining up. He forgot the rule about moving on to fill up spaces and rolled around on the mat during story time for the librarian. Was okay for me but had lots of hands-on activities.*
>
> **Me:** *Thanks for letting me know. I've talked to him about it. It upset him, and he said that he didn't <u>want</u> to be silly (which is good). I hope he is better this week.*
>
> ********
>
> **Teacher:** *CJ was nominated for Aussie of the Week*

for his good behaviour in quiet reading.
Even his classmates noticed how well-behaved he was during this time. Well done!!
Me: *He was very excited about being nominated for Aussie of the week. Thanks*
Teacher: *A good week all round (and she added a 'brilliant' butterfly sticker).*

Schooling years will undoubtedly have ups and downs. Teachers aren't robots and have feelings and problems just like us. Some of CJ's teachers were great with him, and some were just not suited. I'm not blaming anyone for that. Yes, teachers are trained for their job, but personalities are all different, so there are never any guarantees.

If your child has a good year with one teacher, ask them to speak to the following year's teacher to offer suggestions. I found that to be a great help, and then CJ's teacher had a backup person to discuss any issues with, as an alternative to calling me in (phew, thank goodness).

Take an active role at the school where you can. Our kids feel better about going to school if we're a presence there. Show your interest (even if you have little spare time) by helping at the working bee, school fete, reading day, sports day or on an excursion. Help with fundraising, selling chocolates or raffle tickets. Do it together when you can. I joined the school council and helped with an asthma awareness group. I also gave a talk to some of the parents about ADHD in the Parents and Pals group. It all contributed toward CJ's school life and his confidence, not to mention my own confidence!

MEDICATION FOR SCHOOL

Medicating children with ADHD will always bring conflicting opinions, but for CJ medication was the right decision. If you decide on medication don't feel guilty, you're not a bad parent. The benefits (usually) far outweigh any side effects such as sleeplessness and mild appetite loss.

On his Ritalin, CJ could sit still for longer periods. He listened more intently and followed instructions more easily. His silliness went down from fifth gear to first gear, and his handwriting improved dramatically. He was by no means perfect, but for me, that was perfect enough. Just to fit in and get through his day as a happier boy was a great outcome. CJ said he didn't feel much different, but that it was good to not be in trouble so much. (Though a few years later he told me he didn't like taking it because he wasn't funny anymore!)

He took his Ritalin before school and then again at 12 pm. His teacher oversaw this, though now medications would generally be kept at the school office. He was never embarrassed about this as his teacher dealt with it in a positive way. If CJ remembered his tablet first, he scored house points for his team. If a class member remembered first, their team received the house points. There was no teasing as everyone in the class had a chance to be rewarded and looked forward to getting these points. Such a positive way to go about it and it just became a part of the day. (Thank you, Mrs Prescott!)

CJ wasn't medicated forever, just until he learned more self-awareness and better coping methods. He didn't take it on weekends or school holidays unless something was happening that required him to have better concentration or more patience. Now, as an adult, he takes no medication and functions well in his social and working environments.

Repeating a year

We were fortunate in that CJ didn't have to repeat a year, but I would have considered this had it been deemed necessary. He was very intelligent and great with maths and puzzles, but lagged slightly behind his classmates in maturity and other academic areas. He was slow to learn to spell, and his writing was often illegible, but that was something we could work on also at home.

While repeating a grade is never ideal, there are benefits and the earlier that a child is held back if need be, the better. They can gain a head start for the next year and will be better equipped to keep up in class. At lower grade levels, being held back will have a smaller social impact. Instead of feeling a sense of failure they will be likely to fit in with slightly younger children. In a composite grade or in the first two years, it will barely be noticed by the other students. If left until they're older, there will be more self-esteem and social issues to contend with.

CHANGING SCHOOLS

At one point, I seriously considered changing schools for CJ, due to the ongoing problems. I talked to the principal of a neighbouring school who seemed quite positive, and then talked to other parents at that school. Half gave glowing reports, half did not. I truly had no idea what to do so I used the old rule: when in doubt, don't do anything. The more I thought about it I realised that changing schools wouldn't change the problem. His teachers were trying; we just weren't getting it all together quite at that point, so we stayed put.

Most schools are similar: there are nice kids, rowdy kids, good teachers who are very caring and aware, and some not quite as much. I'm grateful that I didn't teach him to run away from problems, but that we should face them head on and work out solutions. The exception may be if a child is diagnosed at a later age, and with the commencement of medication. It may be a good move if they have a well-entrenched reputation as a troublemaker. That can be hard to shake, therefore, a new school, a new outlook; a new beginning may be what they need.

Travel Tips:

- Be a presence, make learning a priority.
- Enlist teachers as allies, not adversaries.
- Use the significant primary years wisely.

17. HOME FRONT HELP

"The best teachers lie within us—within our words, our actions and our example."

Our children spend only a fraction of their days at school, so this is only one part of their education. We play a larger part, and there is much we can do to teach them at home. I remember as a young mum naively thinking 'oh, children should learn everything at school, that's what teachers are for' but I came to see that a child's teacher is just one element of a good education. It's a team effort, and we parents are an important part of that team, especially if a child is struggling with the basics of reading, writing spelling, and maths.

READ AND READ SOME MORE

Often, children will say they don't like to read. It's more that they become disheartened when they're just not 'getting it,' but like most things reading is an acquired skill and requires patience and practice. CJ initially struggled with reading and writing, but he loved when I would read to him, so we always started off with me reading and CJ helping. I often chose books with lessons in them such as *The Grumpies* a book for grumpy kids and *The Berenstain Bear* books, which tackled subjects such as messy rooms and telling lies. (Poor CJ!) With me, almost everything had to be a sneaky lesson, but at that point, he was too young to realise that it was deliberate.

I hoped that CJ would be a reader so to encourage this I also looked for books that he'd really be interested in, mysteries or adventures. I'd read up to a point where CJ just had to know what happened next, and then I'd leave it for him to try for himself. I'd be back to help if he got stuck. It's much easier to get children to read something they are interested in.

Even in today's high-tech world, it's good to go back to basics. Join the library and allow them their own library card. Let them choose their own books. Let them be responsible for marking down on the calendar when they are due back. If they lose interest in a chapter book, try an informative book with shorter sections. We loved the *Giant Book of Questions and Answers* and another called *How Is It Done?*. These were not only great reading but also a great source of learning (I learned a bit too!). Try comic books or joke books, an e-reader or electronic word games; whatever holds their interest. As long as there are words to be read, they are learning!

Incorporate reading and spelling as a part of each day, not just a 'school homework-expectation' at night. When I realised CJ was struggling with reading, I stuck names on everything so he would get to know the words by sight. I labelled each object: 'door,' 'bathroom,' 'drawers,' 'toys'. It didn't really go with the décor, but we got used to it! Be inventive. Try anything that helps.

We can create sneaky reading lessons under the guise of another purpose. Let them cook and use the recipe. This helps not only to read but to measure and follow instructions. Ask them to read you the traffic signs, help look for street signs or get them to read you their school notes when you 'don't have time'.

MAKE WRITING A HABIT

Encourage your child write out their own Christmas cards to friends, thank you notes for gifts or a letter to Nanna. Make reading fun and play old-school educational family games such a *Scrabble* or *Up Words*. Electronic spelling games are another fun way to improve spelling and reading skills. We had a computer game which involved spelling correctly in order to advance through the various levels, but it still had fun themes, spaceships, and funny characters. There were also sneaky writing and spelling lessons under the guise of helping mum. I'd ask CJ to write out one of my famous lists under the pretext of helping me. It may have been a list of things we needed for camp, recipe ingredients or the weekly shopping list.

I'd spell out the words that he didn't know, and then get him to read them back to check that we had everything, at the same time giving him much-needed spelling practise. He could add some things that he would like on the list (okay yes maybe chocolate!) or we would add something silly; after four bananas, I might add "and two monkeys" just to make it more fun.

CJ struggled more with his handwriting than with his reading. By the time he was an avid reader he was still below average when it came to writing. Medication made a huge difference to his hand-eye coordination. His writing was right on track while on the medication, but when it wore off, it could take a painful hour to write five lines, and even then, they weren't very legible. It was very disheartening for him to try his best and see no satisfactory result.

Often, the best time for his homework was right after school while his medication was still working. Aside from that, we asked his teacher for help. She gave us some 'writing homework sheets'. He could trace over pre-written letters for correct shape and sizing. He would first trace them and then try freehand on his own. There was always praise for his attempts. "You've done some good *P's* tonight!" He would circle the ones he thought were the best to monitor himself and be proud of his achievement.

MAKE MATHS FUN

Maths can seem tricky when it doesn't click. In the very early years of school, CJ once commented angrily that 'maths is dumb'. If your child can't figure it out, then maths will seem *dumb* to them. It would be like us getting a few lessons of Chinese each week and then being expected to speak fluently. We might want to give up on it too. If they're not understanding at school, help them at home with visual examples that they can follow. They will have an image in their minds to refer to in future.

Imagine you're making up lolly bags (or is it dried fruit now?) for a birthday party. There are six bags, and we have fifteen lollipops, so how many can we put in each bag to make it even? They can then count it out and see what's left over. There are two lollipops for each bag each with three left over, so that is two and a half times six bags, which makes fifteen lollipops.

Having a physical way to work this out makes it much easier to comprehend. You could then say, "Let's take away the three. How many left?" to practice subtraction (and then eat the leftover lollipops!). Be inventive and apply math's to everyday activities where you can; with saving up weekly pocket money for a goal, for working out change for purchase, or with cutting a birthday cake into portions for the family.

Brush up on the maths that they are learning. Make sure you understand it. I know of one dad (not mentioning any names) who, in trying to be helpful, actually helped his daughter to get the wrong answers to her maths homework. It makes a funny story now, but it wasn't then! Homework can be a rough road and one that will be well travelled, so a routine is a must.

Our kids can be seen as lazy and unmotivated especially with homework, but it's usually more because they are finding it difficult or don't know where to start. A big homework project can seem daunting when it feels like a huge mountain that needs to be climbed. It's easier to *just not try* than to admit they don't know what to do or where to begin. Plan for homework in the daily schedule with a set time, so your child knows when they are expected to work on it and will be prepared. Set aside a time that fits in with your schedule, so you can be there to supervise and keep your child on track until they develop good study habits.

Have them to read over their homework and tell you in their words what they need to do. Check that they understand what's required and help them to organise it into smaller parts. Explain but don't do it for them. (They can sometimes trick us into this!) They might start with a heading and begin the first activity. Once they know what's required, leave them for short intervals then check on their progress. These mini check-ins can help to keep them motivated and on task. Many parents do this already, and that's great, but others may think, "Well, I just did my own when I was their age. They need to be responsible," however with ADHD distractibility, it's a very different story.

If they're still struggling as they get older or if you

find yourself losing patience, consider a tutor. Find one that they will relate to well and enjoy spending time with; maybe a high school or university student (it helps if this person has an abundance of energy!). This can also double as another person in your child's support group, an ally and someone for them to look up to. A little money well spent can take some of the burden off you and also give you an hour of much-needed free time. Win-win again!

Appreciate the primary years; they are by far, the most influential. Then it's off to the diverse labyrinth of high school, a very different experience and another story, but you can only plan ahead so far …

Before I knew it, CJ was almost twelve and his high school years were soon to begin. The Year 7 camp was to be held in the first few weeks, and it was a 'get to know you' camp. I was sure they'd quickly get to know CJ. I knew that his teachers wouldn't be as available to me in high school, now that there were different classes and timetables so wanted to give them a heads up about CJ's ADHD (with an introductory dose of understanding thrown in).

I hoped to come across as approachable as possible in order to enlist their assistance in a positive manner from the start, so I typed up a short note for CJ's Year 7 coordinator and new teachers. My informative, seemingly positive note belied the worry, trepidation and helplessness that I felt when CJ would no longer be close by at his familiar primary school.

This is what I wrote:

Confidential Teacher's Note

Please note that my son CJ has Attention Deficit Hyperactivity Disorder. As you are probably aware, traits of the ADHD child include hyperactivity, inattention, impulsiveness and low self-esteem. Please do not let this diagnosis give you any pre-conceptions.

CJ is doing very well at school so far. He enjoys school (well, as much as an eleven-year-old boy will admit!). He puts effort into his homework and tries as best as he can with other projects. He has a lot of support at home and is quite bright. His handwriting skills still need improving, and he is working on this. CJ is usually well-behaved at school. He is on medication, but we also teach him self-awareness and to be responsible for himself.

We do not use ADHD as an excuse for unacceptable behaviour, but I would ask kindly that it be taken into account (without being made obvious) if any problems should arise. I would be happy at any time meet with CJ's Year 7 teachers to discuss this in more detail if required.

Thanking you for your time,
Mrs Bourke .

But what I really wanted to write was:

Please note that my son CJ has Attention Deficit Hyperactivity Disorder. As you are probably aware, traits of the ADHD child include hyperactivity, inattention, impulsiveness and low self-esteem. He just gets through school, and I am grateful for that. He can be argumentative and can drive me to the brink of insanity at times. He is not always well-behaved at school, and though we teach him self-awareness, he sometimes chooses to ignore it.

He is bright and was awarded the maths prize on the last day of school but was also suspended on the same afternoon ... *I hope he doesn't give you grey hairs whilst on camp and that he doesn't try to swim to China. Please keep an eye on him. I wish I could come to camp with him to be sure another kid won't punch him in the face for annoying them. Please note, he also has a big heart, a great sense of humour and I love him more than anything. Please be nice to him.*

Thanking you for your time,
Mrs Bourke

TRAVEL TIPS:

- Look for the learning in the ordinary.
- Sneaky lessons can double as fun.
- There's no better teacher than you.

18. YOUR FAMILY UNIT

"The invisible assassins of any relationship—pettiness, criticism, resentment, inflexibility
The humble saviours—kindness, respect, generosity understanding
All generated by human choice."

Most days I felt like I was trying to cope with everything myself; ongoing issues with CJ, taking care of Shari and a new baby, teachers, homework, my paid job, helping to run the ADHD support group and volunteering as a parent-to-parent phone contact. Not to mention driving the children to various sports and the not-to-be-forgotten housework. On top of that, my husband Bob, though very hardworking and dependable, displayed some ADHD traits himself (did I mention that?) so he and CJ often had personality clashes. This, in turn, would mean we would all have a personality clash. I'd be trying to defend CJ and at the same time, explain to his dad that his own attitude wasn't helpful, while supposedly trying to keep a united front. And where were our other children in this picture? Taking a back seat, staying out of the way. Not all the time, of course, but take a typical family issue and magnify it by a hundred. That's what we would often end up with, even though it might have begun as a small issue in the first place. Bob was sceptical about his son having the ADHD 'label' put on him, and didn't always deal well with CJ's more frustrating behaviours. When they were good, they were great, but when they weren't, they could be more like adversaries.

One afternoon Bob arrived home from work and CJ was in a mood after another bad day at school. He was complaining about having to do homework because 'that's what school is for!'

I was getting just a bit frazzled, so Bob decided to do the most obvious thing to help ... go fishing. That sounds great you might say. Some bonding with CJ and give me a break to spend time with the other children, but alas, CJ wasn't invited. I told CJ that he wasn't going, but he thought I was joking and that, of course, he must be going. He loved fishing.

CJ watched his dad get the boat ready, having forgotten about the carry-on of not ten minutes ago and was assuming that a night of fishing fun lay ahead. Again, I told him he wasn't going. His dad stomped around hurriedly getting the boat ready, in order to leave the crazy, noisy house for some solitude. Carrying one-year-old Harry, I went out the front to hold onto CJ's hand as he yelled that he wanted to go. His dad, as if making his escape from a menacing tribe of cannibals, slammed the door of the Landcruiser shut, and without looking back, took off down the road. Now in tears, CJ broke free from my grasp and ran down the nature strip after the boat with me following frantically behind (like a scene from a bad comedy movie). I finally caught up with a sobbing CJ and took him home. I was angry, but now, not with CJ. I shook my head in defeat, forgetting about any homework and tried to pick up the remains of the day…

Does that sound like a well-oiled perfectly functioning example of a family dynamic? I would say not, but there went another typical day. When Bob finally came home refreshed, I was still angry with him, and yes, we had words. Don't get me wrong, there were many good days and CJ spent many enjoyable times fishing with his dad, but on this day, things definitely went awry. There was no communication. We were all disjointed, each of us living a different experience of that afternoon in a no-win situation.

Initially, it might sound like all Bob's fault, but I had most likely launched into a rundown of the problems of the day before he even stepped in the door. CJ was probably yelling, and Bob pretty much did what we all would have liked to do, and that was to run away, if only temporarily (I would have if I could have!).

Like many parents, we had conflicting ideas of what discipline entailed and were often at odds with each other. This wasn't because we had a child with

ADHD, but due to the inability to communicate well with each other and due to not operating as a united front. An all-too-common mistake.

Some dads may not accept the ADHD diagnosis; some may spend less time at home. Some may leave all the disciplining to mum and some might reprimand too much. Some mums may feel inadequate (I was), stressed (I was), and begin to lose confidence in their parenting abilities (my hand is raised again!). They start to blame each other and in turn, push each other away. (Swap 'mum' with 'dad' or 'he' with 'she' as you wish in this chapter—either gender can be guilty of these faults)

Compare the next two accounts:

She says: *Everything is up to me; the meetings with the teachers, the frequent paediatrician appointments. I'm either at work or I'm with the kids all day. I have to sort out their fighting, cook, clean and organise everything, and all on top of trying to cope with a hyperactive child that doesn't do a thing I tell him. All my husband has to do is go to work, come home, sit down and do nothing, except maybe have a beer. He won't even spend time with the kids when he gets in; it's straight out to the shed. He says he needs his space. Where's mine? He says I should be more organised, that if I just stopped nagging, I'd be a better mother, that it's not the kids it's me! I do everything now for everybody. It's as if I have three children, not two. There is just no support I feel alone in every way.*

He says: *I can't understand what's happened to her. Before we had the kids, she was so organised, in control, always smiling. Now, all she does is nag and complain. Everything is too much trouble. The minute I get in the door she's at me. Some days I just drive around to prolong going home. She just doesn't realise how demanding my day is, the physical work I have to do, then get my reports written before I finish, not to mention any number of problems that crop up at work. When I get home I need to unwind, relax, not listen to her list of 'terrible things' that the kids have done. They're not bad kids. I wish she'd stop going on about this ADHD thing like it's some disease. I'm sure Sam will grow out of whatever it is eventually. Then she says I have it too. Ridiculous ... and if I did, well I turned out okay anyway. It's as if she expects me to come home and take over everything. That's her job to be a good wife and mother. She used to be happy with that. I don't know why she's complaining now.*

Who's right? Who's wrong? Or are they both right and both wrong? In each case, they believe their partner is unsupportive, and in each case, it's true. Neither is supportive or considerate of the other's feelings. Any good relationship depends on how you make each other feel; be it in a marriage or a friendship, that's a fundamental factor. When you feel loved, appreciated and supported, it's hard to be too unhappy. When you feel unloved, unappreciated and alone, it's easy to be very unhappy. So, what to do? …

Use that scary C word—*communication*! Talk to each other and then talk some more. Yelling isn't talking. Trying to talk with kids yelling isn't talking. Plan a time to talk. Maybe when the children are in bed or before they get home. If need be, talk on the phone. Sometimes that works better! Take down any walls. Get rid of any defences. Keep an open mind.

Listen and acknowledge that you both have valid issues. Try not to interrupt or become defensive. Instead, try to imagine how the other is feeling. It's hard for both of you. Rely on each other for support and validation rather than as an outlet for blame. Compromise if you can't agree. It only takes one person to change an argument into a discussion by being open-minded and reasonable. Be *that person*.

Use respect and understanding and it will be easier to discuss problem issues together instead of trying to outdo each other. "You have no idea how tired I am!" versus "Well, I'm totally exhausted". It's not a competition.

CHOOSE YOUR MAIN CONCERNS

Yes, call them concerns, not complaints, and work out compromises. Maybe dad has half an hour to himself when he walks in the door then he spends time with the children before bed. Maybe mum has a half hour to soak in the bath while dad watches a favourite show with the kids. Be considerate of each other and notice when you are inconsiderate. Agree on rules and future discipline—what goes, what doesn't, what are appropriate punishments and what time is bedtime. When you stick together, discuss, compromise and be consistent, everyone benefits. You'll soon find yourself with an ally and supporter instead of a sounding board that doesn't listen. Look out for each other and be partners in crime. Make a set time to talk about the kids, then close that door and change the subject to relax and unwind.

Many dads have their hands firmly on the wheel, but some can be backseat drivers. They're happy to give an opinion (in conflict with your own) and then leave the rest to you. This can make parenting difficult, but if this is your situation, do your best to include and educate your partner about ADHD in a friendly and supportive way. If they don't like to read an intense, information-packed book, read some main points to them or highlight the most relevant parts. All you can do is try, and if it comes down to it, just do things your way. Explain your reasoning and hopefully your partner will follow suit.

There are also some amazing dads out there that often cope better than mums. They might be the one with more patience for reading and homework, or initiate the fun play and the rough-and-tumble that ADHD children often thrive upon. Pick your strong points and share the load. Don't use the 'wait till your father gets home' threat. It's not fair. He doesn't want to arrive home to be *the bad guy*. Be stronger yourself. Don't let dad always be the enforcer. Fear shouldn't be the motivating factor in promoting good behaviour.

It's up to us to set the scene for our family life and decide what type of life we want. We may not get the 'Brady Bunch', but we can certainly aim for better than the 'Jerry Springer Show'. Even if you've had a bad day, change your attitude for when your partner comes home. Put on a smile and welcoming face. It may be a bit of an act at first, but you can put yourself in any frame of mind when you choose to.

Families come in all shapes and sizes, and through the ADHD support group, I met many single mums. While they didn't have the conflict of disagreements with a partner, they also didn't have that other person there to share the load. A double-edged sword, but the underlying issue was the same as for any other family—support, back-up and validation. Regardless of your situation, it's vital to have that support through friends and family, and a focus on the happiness of yourself and your children.

If you're doing it solo, look for avenues for a time-out for yourself and a mental break. Joining a support group, even if online can bring relief from feelings of isolation and help with strategies and ideas. Friends can be great of course, but they won't all understand the issues, emotions or the degree of difficulty that comes with raising a child with ADHD. Have your support team on hand. Even just a quick call when you need to vent or a few kind words on the computer screen can make all the difference.

SIBLINGS

Our non-ADHD children are often seen as 'the good' ones, the quiet one, the ones that give us little bother. They can be happy to play on their own, do their homework with minimal help and leave us be to contend with our more time-consuming child. While this may seem like a blessing, it took me a while to realise that the lack of complaint from my daughter didn't mean that she was okay. It didn't mean that she didn't resent the disruption to family life because of her older brother's issues. It just meant she was good at taking a back seat, better at controlling her emotions, and that she didn't want to be a burden. I thought that Shari was mature beyond her years. She would just go with the flow, never asked for much, and would often give in so that CJ didn't have a meltdown. But it was taking a hidden toll.

One seemingly ordinary day, Shari came running from her room upset, with CJ following close behind yelling about something. (I still to this day, have no idea what about!) She looked distraught, but when CJ caught up with her, she suddenly stopped and turned to him, as if in resignation. As if deciding enough was enough, she grabbed her big brother furiously by the arm and like a competitor in a world championship wrestling match, spun him around and around, then let go, catapulting him into the lounge room wall. Everything went still and seemed to be in slow motion. I was shocked. Shari looked shocked and CJ even more shocked. This all happened in a few seconds, and I expected a quick retaliation. To my total surprise, CJ got up, unhurt except for his pride and quietly went back to his room.

Unsurprisingly, that was my biggest and most obvious indication as to how Shari really felt. Though she seemed happy-go-lucky, in reality, she felt that everything revolved around CJ and that she was overlooked. In her own little way, she had been stressed too, but she was trying to deal with it herself, not wanting to be a burden.

My three children were equally as important as each other, and I had to ensure that they all knew it. Even if my expectations were a little different, I had to ensure they all felt loved and valued. Harry was an easygoing, happy child, and much younger than his siblings so fortunately he was oblivious to many issues. But at times both Harry and Shari missed out on things, like a calm atmosphere or just my undivided attention. This needed to become another focus. It's easy to forget that our other children need validation also and they may misbehave to gain attention if this isn't recognised.

I wanted to ensure that Shari and Harry, as he grew older, had a good understanding of CJ's ADHD traits. Not as a negative, but as an addition to his personality and so he wasn't seen to get away with things that they wouldn't dare try, such as yelling or talking back. It was important that they understood I wasn't being harder on them, just more accepting of their brother's impulsive ADHD behaviours. It gave them an opportunity to learn compassion and understanding beyond their years. They understood that CJ needed his tablet (Ritalin) to help him concentrate and if he hadn't taken it, they became more patient with him even though they were the younger siblings. I made more effort to praise Shari and Harry for being well-behaved, realising that they may not feel appreciated as much for the things they just did naturally. I made an effort not to simply expect them to be the more sensible ones. They were children too.

It's important not to compare siblings, but to accept their individual needs, strengths and weaknesses. Saying, "Why can't you be more like your sister?" or "If you don't behave, Charlotte can choose the TV shows" only promotes jealousy and rivalry. We want them to look out for each other, not the opposite. Rather, we can encourage siblings to see each other's good points and to appreciate each other. "Shari always shares her pencils with you," or "It was great that CJ helped you through the next level of the video game". We can remind them that their efforts are appreciated with phrases like, "CJ, that was nice of you to teach Harry how to ride the skateboard". We can help our children to 'work as a team' and to include each other where possible.

It's important not to use flippant labels and to watch our attitude toward our ADHD child in front of siblings. We might make offhand remarks like, "Gosh, Amy's being a pain today," or "Tom makes me so mad sometimes!" Their siblings might then wonder what we say about them when they're not around. It also may encourage them to believe that the ADHD child isn't a valuable member of the family and treat them poorly.

The little things that we say offhandedly are sometimes the things that stick and are carried through to adulthood. I remember my mum introducing me as 'the shy one', and that's what I became. It could be 'the silly one', 'the good one', 'the clever one' or 'our little terror'. Give a negative label and you will usually get a negative child. Children can also worry about living up to our expectations. When given the 'clever' or 'good' labels children can become anxious that they might let us down. We want our children to know that a parent's love is unconditional, and they don't have to be ashamed if they make mistakes or have a bad day, no matter which child it may be. Each of our children were often given a 'special' job to help out with, so they felt important and appreciated within the family. CJ liked to help to wash the car, especially using the hose! Shari liked to help with the ironing (apparently ironing is fun when you're a kid!). Harry liked to help with anything at all, even folding the laundry.

When it comes to sibling squabbles, it's

important not to lay blame just because our ADHD child is the usual suspect. They can easily become the scapegoat. If Shari had a friend over, the girls might have come running to me, exclaiming "CJ did this. CJ did that," and often I would fall hook, line and sinker. What I didn't realise was that a lot of time he wasn't the instigator. He was just the one getting told on because; yes, girls can be dibber-dobbers and enjoy getting boys into trouble, thus being seen as 'the good ones'.

If I was unsure of the situation or who the real culprit was, there was a remedy that worked well. The children were sent to play in their rooms. I'd tell them that I didn't want to hear who started it, but that they could come out as soon as they were ready to make up with each other, and I didn't want to know whose fault it was. It was incredible how fast a cease-fire would occur, and they'd be allowed out again. In doing this, they could be allies together against mum—and that's okay too.

SANITY SAVERS

We can get stuck in one pattern of thinking and forget to explore other ways of doing things. We can get into a rut and relive the same issues day after day. For a time, every morning we would have the same squabbles at breakfast time. It was as if someone rang a bell and said, "Go for it. Time starts now!" And it would begin … who was on the best stool, who had the most room, whose feet are in whose space. CJ would yell, Shari would retaliate, and I'd feel my stress levels rising (Happy Harry would smile at everyone from his high chair as if greatly amused). Day after day we went through this same ritual, all the while hoping things would improve. Occasionally they did, and I would praise my children, but they soon returned to the same silly squabbles. Until one morning I thought, "Why do we continue to do this day after day? Breakfast time is a pain for all of us at the moment, so let's change that." I then got rid of the 'they should be able to sit happily together' mentality and decided to do what worked for everyone ... so they had breakfast separately.

It wasn't a big deal as, usually, one woke before the other and I got to spend a few minutes alone with each of them to chat about the day ahead. Alternatively, if it was a pleasant morning, we might all have breakfast outside. Fresh air works wonders, and with the morning dew, and the birds singing, it's hard for anyone to be grumpy, myself included.

We minimised the squabbles that once dominated our mornings just by doing what worked for us. They didn't know this was done on purpose. It looked like an innocent coincidence, but it limited the fighting, and it wasn't forever. Eventually, they came to like each other's company, but until then we did it our way.

When there's been much disruption to the daily lives of our other children, ensure siblings know that their patience is appreciated, and acknowledge that they do take a back seat at times. Check that they're okay and be ready to listen when they're not. Thank them when they handle a situation well. Don't just expect them to always be the 'good ones'. Make special time for them. Treat them on their own when you can, be it taking one on their own for new shoes or bringing one home early from school to pack for camp. It doesn't have to be anything dramatic, just enough to make them feel special. Encourage that united front and work together for the same aim: a stable, loving family unit (with just a touch of chaos at times!).

FAMILY COUNSELLING

"Surely, we must be crazy if we need to see a psychologist!" This is a common misconception but think about it. If your child were having problems with their vision, you would take them to an optometrist; problems with their teeth you would see the dentist. It follows that, for on-going behavioural problems, you would consult a psychologist. They are the experts in human behaviour and on human behavioural change. Counselling and advice can be provided, not only to assist your ADHD child, but to strengthen the family as a whole. Some parents have a good grasp on how to manage their child's behaviour, but many find it a daily struggle. It is not a character flaw and doesn't mean that you're a *bad* parent. Few of us are prepared for so-called normal parenting, let alone the parenting of a child with ADHD.

They don't come with an instruction book and we learn through trial and error. (Though there are now many helpful books on the market!) Some parents will benefit considerably from the more personal guidance that a psychologist can give and that's nothing to be ashamed of. Just as you'd visit a family doctor for any other ailment, treat a visit to the psychologist in the same way.

TRAVEL TIPS:

- Look from more than one perspective.
- Listen for what you don't always hear.
- Ensure the 'good' siblings feel valued too.

19. RECLAIMING THE BOND

"Distance dissolves when we set the weather for a relationship from cloudy with possible storms, to sunny with clear skies—taking along a shared umbrella for unexpected downpours."

CJ was almost eight when he was diagnosed with ADHD, so before knowing there was an underlying issue, I was easily frustrated and annoyed with CJ's more irritating behaviours. It may have been the constant bickering with his younger sister (baby brother Harry wasn't old enough to fight with yet) or when he insisted on being in the front seat of the car when it wasn't his turn, or when he had to have the first go of anything. And yes, all children do this, but not quite so relentlessly! It may have been when he persistently argued back with me, or when he'd run off from me without a second's notice, or when he'd attempt to climb onto his Auntie's roof with a huge grin and no ladder.

I'd compare him with other children with more sensible behaviours and easy-going natures, and I'd feel resentful. This became apparent in my attitude of generally expecting the worst. In turn, he became more defiant rather than compliant, and a roadblock was formed, hampering the close bond we once had. I saw this closeness gradually slipping away, like a leaf floating downstream with nothing to stop it.

With the knowledge that ADHD was the main culprit, not an excuse but the underlying factor, I realised that CJ wasn't just deliberately being naughty or disruptive. In his eyes, he was just doing what came naturally, but getting in trouble for most of it. It was time to retrieve my sweet child from behind that tough exterior. It was time to forgive CJ for his perceived *bad* behaviour, and to forgive myself for thinking he was *just naughty*, for not seeing his struggle, but seeing only my own.

Along the way, he'd become accustomed to feeling bad about himself, so it was time to reverse that. In hindsight, I could see that his errors of judgement were often accidental or incidental and not made with any bad intention. Like the time he and little brother Harry sped through the house both dressed as Ninjas in matching blue dressing gowns with pretend weapons tucked into their belt.

From my view, all I saw was ten-year-old CJ on top of three-year-old Harry 'stabbing' him with a wooden ruler. Who knew that rulers were really pretend swords and that Harry was a more-than-willing blue ninja participant until he fell over. Impatient mum then appears, and afraid of being in trouble yet again, CJ yells to protest his innocence, making him look even more guilty to this clueless mum. It was this impulsiveness and lack of vocal restraint that got him into trouble the most, but CJ wasn't just a challenging child. He was a great little boy who brought us love and laughter, just as our other children did. He lived by a different set of internal rules and guidelines, but that didn't mean he was always in the wrong. He often saw things differently, but it was no one's fault, not his, nor mine; and it was long overdue that I reclaimed our close relationship. So, where to start…

THE BEST MEDICINE

Imagine if your doctor said, "I'd like to tell you about something very special. It's something that will raise your child's spirits, boost their self-esteem, create happy memories and give you both a better relationship. It's guaranteed and will only cost a one-off payment of $99!"

We'd all want some of that wonderful thing and would try to come up with that $99 as soon as we could. The good news is we already have that wonderful thing at our disposal, and the best news is that it's free! So, what is this wonderful thing? It's 'time'—time spent with our children enjoying their company. And this was where I had to begin.

Admittedly there were times I would have preferred to be as far away as possible from the defiant Master CJ as possible, but if I wanted our relationship back on track, I had to go back to basics. I had to reacquaint myself with the little person inside; the real little person with feelings, insecurities, hopes and dreams, just like we all have. I had to take the time to understand how his mind worked and make the time to get to know him again.

It's surprising how we think we have no extra time then something becomes a priority, and we just make it happen. Like when an old friend calls with an invitation to lunch, or a cancellation at the dentist. They can suddenly fit you in, and abracadabra, it's done! It all depends on how much *we want* to find this time. We all have different schedules and responsibilities, and there might not seem little time for the much debated 'quality time,' but we can make it happen, even if we start small. We're busy running from here to there, working, shopping, going to the gym, taking children to different activities; but like a suitcase, if we plan and pack our time wisely, we can make more room to fit things in, even at the most unlikely of times.

It doesn't take too much effort on our part to make this time 'quality time'. We can take advantage of *any time* we have with our children, be it driving in the car, waiting at the dentist or just having a meal together These are the best times to talk about their day (as they can't escape!), to tell them about our day, and to help them feel included.

Slot it into the family routine. We would have a mini family quiz at dinner time with everybody joining in, or 'good news' time when the kids could only talk about something good that happened in their day. I'd have to think of something as well, so it was also a great way to teach appreciation. We played simple card games together, like *Thirty-One,* a game suitable for most ages that could take as little as ten minutes or as long as you wish. Another card favourite was *Uno* when there was more time.

Plan ahead and set aside this time, even just a half hour spent with you will be special to your child. Not *maybe later*, as the elusive *later* may never come. Make this time a priority then relax and enjoy the ride. Keep an activities list of things that that can be used especially for these times. Children can give input when choosing activities (within guidelines) to help them feel responsible and valued. It might be an Xbox race-off with them, or making dolls clothes from old socks, or as simple as a game of *Scrabble* or other board game (not *Monopoly* though … I was a bad loser at monopoly, and CJ was a notorious cheat!). It might be a kick of the footy at the local oval, a walk with the dog, a bounce on the trampoline, a funny movie or baking a cake together. Maybe a bit of fun play, like a water gun fight, a silly dance-off, or in this photo-crazy world some funny selfies together. We can all use a little silliness sometimes. Find something mutually agreeable for everyone or pick one out of a hat. And okay, our ADHD child might complain if their choice isn't the one chosen, so let him be the one to pick out of the hat and read it out.

It's great to have a whole family activity or interest—something that binds you together. It might just be a regular comedy movie night with homemade popcorn (and no phones or devices allowed) or watching the football and placing tips on who might win together. CJ, Shari and Harry loved fishing, boating and swimming, so we were often out in the boat for family-time. At home, we enjoyed the Nintendo game 'Super Mario'. Being a multiplayer game, there were no arguments about whose turn it was. When your character dies you're done, and you just have to wait; but it's also fun to watch the other players as well. (We still have that game to this day, and more Mario games have come along, encouraging the same type of teamwork.) They couldn't get their dad to play video games, but he was the fishing guru, so they let him off that hook.

MEMORIES OF A MOMENT

Often the best memories are from the simple moments that come with spending just a short time together. There was the time we played cricket together in the backyard and accidentally smashed the shed window. CJ remembers us as partners in crime that day, a special bond of sorts. That day we played together for only twenty minutes. A small price for the memories it brought. Oh ... and the price of the window.

One Friday evening, while I was at work, there was a large grass fire at the end of our street. There were helicopters, fire trucks and TV news cameramen, but I'd missed it by the time I arrived home just after 9 pm. CJ was, of course, still wide awake and was enthusiastically telling me about the excitement of the day. The fire was still smouldering so there were still fire engines in the street and CJ asked if we could walk down in the dark for a look. Without thinking, 'no' was my spontaneous answer: "It's way past your bedtime, never mind that I've just gotten home and want to sit down".

"Please, can we?" he pestered. I then remembered the advice I would give to anyone else. A little grudgingly I agreed, and with CJ in pyjamas and dressing gown, we walked to the end of the street. The fire was still bright against the dark night sky. CJ was excited, and I could tell he felt special to be out so late. He asked a firefighter a quick fifty questions, and we watched them refill their water from the roadside hydrant before walking home. This all took around twenty minutes—not long at all. Back at home, I said that it must have been a very eventful day with the helicopters and fire trucks, and I asked him what his favourite part was. Still excited, he replied, "The best part was the walk in the dark with you". I could see he truly meant that and it warmed this tired mum's heart. I realised how little effort it had taken to create this great memory and how it's often when we least expect it.

Another night CJ kept getting up out of bed. He hadn't done this for a while, and I was annoyed at not having my free time. I was 'busy' watching TV. When I thought about it, I realised that most nights he was good at bedtime so there must be something wrong. He wasn't saying much and couldn't give me a reason, but maybe he just needed that little bit of extra attention. I told him he could sit up with me and that he had fifteen minutes. He asked if we could read a bit from a book we kept in the study, full of interesting facts.

We enjoyed the reading together and went a little over time, but I was then able to send him to bed satisfied that he was important. It could have been another run of the mill night, with me yelling 'get to bed' another five or six times and taking up the same amount of time as the reading, but not so enjoyable. He remembered that night as something special, for a small fifteen-minute (okay maybe twenty-five-minute) effort on my part. This wasn't every time though. If it were every time, he would just come to expect it. It made such a difference to surprise CJ with an unexpected kindness that he may not have deserved. The difference to his mood and self-esteem was a reward for me and another step in bringing us closer.

KEEP UP THE CONNECTION

Our kids can feel hurt, overwhelmed, not good enough or just upset for being so often *in trouble*. A few minutes spent to encourage them to talk can make all the difference. They might clam up, but with some gentleness and coaxing they might also open up.

When CJ couldn't sleep, and something was on his mind, maybe a bad day with friends or in trouble with dad, we would have a chat. And no, his angry little self often didn't want to chat, but we had a way around that. Even when he wouldn't talk to me, he would talk to a particular green furry friend.

Mr Crocodile was a puppet who, like CJ, was 'made' in 1987. To CJ, this meant a special bond. Mr Crocodile also doubled as the tickle monster, with me as the chaser and CJ and Shari as the 'chase-ees'. But at night, if CJ seemed down, I'd slip Mr Crocodile onto my hand and ask in my best crocodile voice, about what was bothering him. CJ would look into the glass eyes of his crocodile companion, and as if I wasn't there, he would tell Mr Crocodile his thoughts and troubles. Mr Crocodile was great at asking questions and giving advice (if I say so myself!) and a troublesome day could still end happily with Mr Crocodile soon becoming tired, yawning and snuggling in beside CJ. I was then free to go, safe in knowing that I'd left CJ in good, albeit crocodile, hands.

USE THE RESPECT YOU EXPECT

Respect is the unseen barrier that keeps us in check. It stops us from saying and doing things that damage our relationships, but it is often overlooked and not always actively on the agenda. When our ADHD children blurt things out inappropriately, misbehave or yell, we tend to see this as a lack of respect when it is more a lack of control. If we reciprocate in the same way, we're just giving the same lack of respect that we want to discourage. We can all turn into that angry saboteur when we least expect it and say things we don't mean. This happens, but it shouldn't be the daily way to converse. Imagine if we bluntly corrected a good friend every time we thought they were wrong, or when we didn't like their opinion. Imagine if we constantly criticised a friend when we thought we knew better, or just yelled at them when we were annoyed.

No, Tracey, that's not how you make the dip! Haven't I told you a million times not to use basil? Seriously, Linda, will you just hurry up; you always make us late! Oh, wow, Caroline, you drank the last glass of the wine? What! No cashews left either? Right, that's it, Caroline! Don't come over again for a week! (Okay maybe not quite those words, but you get the picture.)

We wouldn't have those friendships for very long. While we may not agree with everything our friends say or do, we respect them enough to use care with our words when giving our opinions. We can use this same respect with our children, regardless of the situation, no matter how frustrated we may become. We can correct with patience and kindness and keep criticisms to a minimum so as to not hurt little feelings and to retain that close bond. Of course, there'll be times when we get grumpy, impatient and angry. We're only human. But we can always aim for better.

You may already do these things and more, and that's fantastic, but many other parents struggle to retain a close connection. We all love our children, it goes without saying, but that can be the problem—it often goes without being said. In our busy lives, we can assume it speaks for itself. It doesn't take a lot to enable a child to feel loved and valued for who they are. A little of our time, an 'I love you' and a hug, even when they're misbehaving, can turn a day and a life, around.

Often, on a bad day, instead of seeing it for what it was (just a bad day), I would make problems so much larger in my mind. I would imagine all sorts of future issues. I'd be worried about tomorrow, about CJ's future. Will he get suspended, maybe even expelled? Will he end up with the wrong crowd or take off and I'll never see him again? Or what if he went to jail? And this was only year three!

This pointless worry impacted my attitude, and I had to tell myself. "Stop. He's only eight!" I didn't need to imagine ten years down the track and get all worked up.

All I had to do was spend a little time now to help him feel loved, valued and respected; and with a little luck thrown in, the future would take care of itself.

TRAVEL TIPS:

- Create time to make positive changes.
- Use the respect you come to expect.
- Clear roadblocks with an open, caring attitude.

20. A FINAL WORD

Though the road ahead may not always seem clear, never lose sight of your destination.

It's easy to get caught up in the day-to-day *small stuff because* it becomes hard. It's hard when we feel disrespected, undermined, and as if we're failing as parents. It's hard when we continually doubt ourselves and feel like giving up. It's hard to see our children being 'in trouble' and not coping. We can think we've done all that we can and end up feeling defeated. But if you're reading this book and have come this far, you are by no means defeated. You've picked yourself up, dusted yourself off and are continuing on—so good job! It can seem overwhelming, but everything does pass. It can seem as if the diagnosis of ADHD is a life sentence, a continual *Groundhog Day*, going over and over the same battles, stuck in one place, but you will move forward. Believe it or not, these early years are the easiest and the most influential. When the teenage years hit, that's another story on its own. (Perhaps another few volumes!)

The groundwork you put in now will greatly benefit those future teenage years. Our children are not children forever. They're with us for a short period of time compared to the length of our entire life, so use these childhood years wisely. Time seems to move slowly, but only until we look back on it. Then we realise it just ran away, like the dish with the spoon.

It can be hard to change firmly entrenched behaviours, both for ourselves and our children, but when we push ourselves repeatedly to do things in a certain way, they soon become habits and habits are easy to continue. Great life changes are often made in the small details: being open-minded, listening better, understanding more, a child trusting in you to always be there for them, and to always believe in a child with unconditional love.

I have included a lot of 'bad' stories in this book, but only to show that 'normal' comes in many shapes and sizes. Some are part of the normal parenting spectrum, but other examples, well not so much. Many 'regular' parents might say, "Wow, that's nuts! How could you let things get that far?" But most don't understand our kids can go from zero (being a normal day) to one hundred (in the *danger zone)* in just minutes, catching us off guard. They can say things and do things other children wouldn't dream of doing or saying. Like suddenly swearing at a teacher or slamming the door in a visiting cousin's face. Like bringing home and echidna in a basket because he 'found it' on the side of the road, and like going possum hunting with a fishing net and actually bringing home a possum (promptly followed by on an impromptu hike with mum to return it to its home!). But as well as tumultuous times, there were also wonderful times with much joy, laughter and happy unpredictability.

As you have seen, I love my lists. They kept me on track. You could say this book is one big list. It began with me jotting down 'ADHD things to remember'. When you find things that work for you, jot them down for future reference. I used an exercise book, but it can be on your phone or iPad, whatever suits. By no means do I profess to have all the answers. I am no expert. I deliberately haven't included any dietary or medical advice, as this should be discussed individually with appropriate health professionals.

Take from my experiences what suits you, leave behind what doesn't. This book is written based on my own trials, errors and successes, and while I have used examples from our family life, they are just that, examples. This book is not only about my son, but about all of our challenging children, and for the benefit of all of our families. It is written with the best of intentions to help others who are struggling now, as I was in those early years. In sharing with you, some of my insight, experiences, and hindsight; my hope is that you will find your own answers; answers that work for you and your family.

When children have encountered much negativity, be it either at school, at home, or in any social setting, they soon become accustomed to being seen as the 'naughty one'. They become immune to the disapproval of others, and over-used threats and punishments lose their effectiveness. We can find alternatives that not only save our sanity but bring out the best in our children. They're not *just naughty*. They're beautiful, irreplaceable individuals that just happen to drive us crazy at times!

They may have their own unique mannerisms; they may live by their own steadfast principles and see the world from a different perspective, a world that doesn't cater well for what's not seen to be 'normal'. But who's to say what's normal and what's not. They have the traits we admire in the leaders, the thinkers and entrepreneurs of the world. These traits may not seem so endearing in children, but can be channelled and encouraged. These qualities have served CJ well as an adult in the workforce, getting him to where he is today.

There were many ups and downs during the high school years with different sets of issues to overcome, but eventually he went on to finish his schooling and complete an apprenticeship. He soon decided this trade was not for him, and with no fear of failure, went on to pursue his dream career as a crane driver. Today CJ is a competent young man, working in his chosen field, with children of his own. He has ups and downs just like anyone else, and is making his way in the world. He is still unique, with a love of tattoos that I can't quite say I share! He and his dad worked out their differences (and similarities!) and have become best mates. He and

Harry are also best mates, and he has a good relationship with Shari despite them being polar opposites. He and I are still close. This was the destination I had hoped for, a destination that may seem an ordinary road in life to many others, but not one to be taken for granted.

When I began writing this book, I stopped many times, thinking people would judge me, that they would say, "Oooh" and, "Ah" or "Oh, I wouldn't have done that!" But none of that matters. What matters is that we each work out our own route, work out our own metaphorical roadmap. It may not be the road others would choose. It may seem off the beaten track, but whatever works for you, your child and your family is the right path.

It's important not to judge each other as parents. We each have our own mini-universe in our individual homes, and what works for one won't necessarily work for the other. Rather, we need to support each other and respect our differences, and at the same time, learn from each other. We all have similar, yet different stories. We all love our children dearly and want the best for them. We all make mistakes on the journey that is raising our children, but those mistakes will only become our regrets if we fail to learn the lessons that they hold. Don't give up, don't lose hope. Hope is free and hope is a choice, just like any other.

Let any divided road end here; with you and your child beginning the next leg of the journey together.

The road may be bumpy. It may have twists and turns. You may experience a few crashes and need repairs along the way, but with love and understanding, kindness and humour, you *will* reach your destination.

FINAL TRAVEL TIPS:

- Enjoy and appreciate your wonderfully unique child.
- Enjoy and appreciate the ever-changing journey ahead.
- Believe in yourself to create your own personal roadmap.

ADHD PARENTING

We have all the ingredients within us, but sometimes misplace the recipe.

Keep trying, testing and adjusting, until you find your 'just right' blend.